Body Language and Nlp

Dark Psychology Master's Guide to a comprehensive Study of Mind Control, Persuasion, People Analysis, and Brainwashing (2022 Crash Course for Beginners)

Urban Reyes

1

TABLE OF CONTENTS

INTRODUCTION

The field of dark psychology repreents human beings' ability to engage n dark practce that hearken to motvaton that are poorly masters of the dark pychologcal art are adept at readng other people, they are also klled at uckly establishing m Reader will learn how to analyze other that mater manpulator do in Dark Pychology Secrets and the rt of Reading People.

Some experts have a high level of ability to decipher others' thoughts, emotions, and other external characteristics. Reading people enables you to determine the truth, emotional state, intentions, and even romantc nteret. though most people engage n readng other to ome degree, readng other people accurately a knowledge that often lap through our grap We spend a lot of our time worrying about how we interact with others. If we can connect and communicate effectively, we can move through life more efficiently. Of coure, everyone else would be a lot earther if everyone else walked like us, right?

Reading People I a very ueful system for quickly determnng the type of peron you're engagng wth and how to get the better out You will learn how to communicate with others in ways that elicit positive responses, as well as how to avoid minor misunderstandings. This is an effective way to gain a deeper understanding of yourself, become aware of some of your blind spots, and celebrate your inherent strength.

Reading People exports the pattern that different types of people naturally adapt when they nteract wth other types of people. It's also a powerful way to communicate with your students in their native language in a simple and effective manner. lthough manpulaton and mand control are motvaton that spur ome people to hone there kill at reading others, the ability to read others give

1. Create a Baseline

People have different quirks and behavor patterns. For example, they may clear throat, look at the flood when talking, cratch their head, troke their neck, pout, or juggle. In general, we may not even notice when others engage in these behaviors. We don't pay much attention to it if we do. These behaviors are displayed by people for a variety of reasons. They may simply be mannerisms. However, these actions can be ndcatve of decepton, anger, or nervousness.

Making a mental model of other people's normal behavior will assist you...

2. Look for Deviations

Take note of the ncontence between the baelne you've made and the person's words and gestures. As an example, you've noticed that an important supplier of yours has a habit of clearing h throat repeatly when nervous. He tarts to do as he introduces some relatively small change to your business arrangement. Is there anything else here than meet the eye? You may decde to probe for a few more ueton than you would have have have have have have have have have have have

3. Notice Geture Clusters

No lone geture or word needly mean anything, but take note when every behavoral aberraton clumped together. For example, your uppler not only keep clearng heart, but he alo does that head-cratchng thng. And he kept shuffle-shuffle-shuffle-shuffle-shuffle-shuffle-shuffle-shu

4. Contrast and compare

Okay, so you've noticed that someone is acting a little strangely. Move your obervation up a notch to ee f and when that peron repeated the ame behavior with other n your group

Continue to watch the individual as he or she interacts with others in the room. Is it possible for a person's experience to change? What about her poture and body language?

5. Look at Yourself in the Mirror

Mirror neurons in our brain are built-in monitors that reflect the mental state of others. We are expected to read each other's body language. mle actvate our mle mucle, whereas a frown actvate our frown mucle. When we see someone we like, our eyebrows arch, our facial muscles relax, our heads tilt, and blood flows to and fills our leps. If your partner does not reciprocate, that peron may endng you a clear meage: He or she dislikes you or is unhappy with something you've done.

6. Recognize trouble Voice

The most powerful person is not always at the head of the table. Confidential people have hard voices. Around a conference table, the most confident person is almost always the most powerful:

- Expansive poture, trong voce, and a big smile. (Do not mix up a loud voice with a strong one.)
- If you're pitching an idea to a group, it's simple to pay attention to the team leader. However, that leader may have a weak peronalty. In reality, he or she is heavily reliant on others to make decisions and is easily influenced by them.

- Identfy the trong voce, and your chance for ucce ncreae dramatcally.

7. Observe How They Walk

Frequently, people who huffle along, lack a flowng motion n their movements or keep their head down lack self-confidence. If you notice thee traits in a member of your team, you may make an extra effort to offer commendation, to help, build the person's confdence You may need to ak her more drect ueton dure a meeting, to pull the great ideas out nto the open.

8. Pinpoint action Words

As an FBI agent, I discovered that words were the simplest way for me to get into another person's head. Word reprent thoughts, to identify the word freghted wth meanng. For example, if your boss says she's "decided to go with brand X," the action word is decided. This single word ndcate that your boss most lkely

- Is not mpulve
- Weighed several options
- Consider things carefully.

Action words offer insights into how a person thinks.

9. Look For Peronalty Clues

Each of you has a unique personality, but there are basic classifications that can help you relate to another person so you can read him or her accurately.

- Does one exhbt more introverted or extroverted behavor?
- Does he or she appear to be driven by relatonhp or gnfcance?
- How does the person handle rak and uncertanty?
- What did he or her ego feed?

- What are the peron's behavor when treed?
- What are the person's behavors when relaxed?
- Putting it all together

all the time, This advice made me think. he acknowledge, it take to learn how to reactly reactly reactly reactly reactly reactly reactly reactly reactly re And, of course, there are exceptions to every rule. Keeping these principles in mind as you build your power of observation will greatly improve your ability to read others, understand their thoughts, and communicate effectively.

CHAPTER 1:

NON VERBAL COMMUNICATION

A significant portion of our communication is nonverbal. Xperts have found that every day we repond to thouands of nonverbal cue and behavor ncluding poture, facial expressions, eye gaze, gestures From our hartyle to our handshakes, nonverbal cues reveal who we are and influence how we relate to others.

What Is Non-Verbal Communication

Non-Verbal Communcation (NVC) the tranmon of messages or gnal through a nonverbal platform such as eye contact, facial expressions, It ncludes the ue of vual cues such as body language (knec), distance (proxemics), and phycal envronment/ appearance, voce (paralanguage), and touch (haptics). It can also include the use of time (chronemics) and eye contact, as well as the action of looking while talking and listing, the frequency of glances, pattern of fixation, pupl dlaton, and blink rate (oculesics).

Nonverbal communication involves both conscious and unconscious processes of encoding and decoding. nCoding is the act of generatng nformation uch a facial expressions, geture, and poture. ncodng nformation utlze gnal, which we may thnk to be unveral Decoding the nterpretation of nformation from receved sensations given by the encoder Decoding nformation utlize knowledge one may have of certanly received enaton.

For example, the encoder holder up two fnger, and the decoder may know from prevou experence that that meant two.

Culture plays an important role in nonverbal communication, and it is one aspect that influences how learning activities are organized. For example, in many Indenou mercan communte, there is often an emphasis on nonverbal communcaton, whch acts as a valued mean by whch children lea In thene, learnng is not depended on verbal communication; rather, it is nonverbal communication that erve a prmary mean of not only organzng nterperonal

What Is Nonverbal communication?

Nonverbal communication is the transfer of nformation through the ue of body language ncluding eye contact, facial expreon, geture, and more. Verbal communcation the ue of language to tranfer information through written text, peakng, or sign language

Nonverbal communication is important because it provides us with valuable information about a situation, such as how a person is feeling, how someone receives information, and how to approach a person. Paying attention to and developing the ability to read nonverbal communication is a valuable skill that you can develop at any stage of your career.

Nonverbal Communication Types

There are several types of nonverbal communication that you should be aware of, including:

1. Body Language: Body language is the natural way that someone positions their body depending on the situation, the environment, and how they are feeling. For example, if a person is angry or nervous, they may cro their arms. Consider how your perceptions of people are influenced by the way they t, walk, tand, or hold their head. The way you move and carry yourself communicates a wealth of information to the rest of the world. Nonverbal communication includes your posture, bearing, tance, and the subtle movements you make.

2. Geturé: While gestures vary widely across communities, they are commonly used to convey information to others, both intentionally and unintentionally. For example, n the United State, someone may display a "thumb up" to communicate confrmation or that they feel positive about omething. Consider how your perception of people is influenced by the way they t, walk, stand, or hold their heads. The way you move and carry yourself communicates a wealth of information to the world. This type of nonverbal communication includes your posture, bearing, tone, and the smallest movement you make.

3. Fecal expression: Facial expression is one of the most common forms of nonverbal communication. When communicating both emotions and information, using the eyebrows, mouth, eyes, and facial muscles can be very effective. The human face is extremely expressive, capable of conveying complex emotions without saying a single word. facial expressions

13

are unveral, lke other form of nonverbal communication. The facial expreon for happne, sadness, anger, urpre, fear, and disgust acro cultures are the same.

4. Touch: Some people use touch as a form of communication as well.

It is most commonly used to communicate support or comfort. This form of communication should be used sparingly and only when you know how the receiving party feels about you. It should never be used to convey anger, frustration, or any other negative emotions in the workplace. We communicate a great deal through touch. Consider the very different messages conveyed by a weak handshake, a warm bear hug, a patronzng pat on the head, or a controllng grip on the arm, for example

5. eye contact: Because the verbal ene is dominant for most people, eye contact an especially more more more more more more more more more more more mor Many things can be communicated by the way you look at someone, including nteret, affecton, hotlty, or attraction. Ye contact also maintains the flow of converation and for gaugng the other peron's interest and reponse.

6. Space: Have you ever felt uneasy during a meeting because the other person was standing too close and invading your space? We all need phycal pace, though that need depends on the culture, the situation, and the cloene of the relation. You can use physical space to communicate a variety of nonverbal messages, including signs of ntmacy and affecton, aggression, or dominance.

7. VOICE: It's not just what you say, but also how you say it. When you speak, other people "read" your voice in addition to listening to your words. Things they pay attention to include your timing and space, how loud you speak, your tone and nflecton, and sounds that convey understanding, such as "ahh" and "uh-huh."

Consider how your tone of voice can ndcate arcam, anger, affecton, or confidence.

HOW TO READ BODY LANGAUGE

Reading body language is a difficult skill that you will continue to develop throughout your career. While each person uses nonverbal communication differently, there are several common cues to pay attention to that will inform you about a person's feelings, thoughts, and motivation. When communicating with someone, it's helpful to notice their body language while also taking in their verbal communication. Once you've honed your ability to manage tremors and recognize emotions, you'll begin to improve your ability to read nonverbal messages sent by others. It is also critical to

1. Pay attention To Incontence: Nonverbal communication should reinforce what is being said. Is the person saying one thing, but their body language is conveying something else? For example, are they telling you "yes" while shaking their head no?

Examine nonverbal communication signals as a group. Don't read too much into a single geture or nonverbal cue. Consider all of the nonverbal cues you are receiving, from eye contact to voice tone and body language. Taken together, their noverbal cue

content or ncontent wth what their word are saying?

2. Trust your Instinct: Don't ignore your gut instincts. If you get the feeling that someone isn't being heard or that something isn't adding up, you might be picking up on a match between verbal and nonverbal cues.

Here are few ues f body language that you can begn to look for:

1. Poture: If a peron ha ther houlder back and pne traght, they are engaged, lenng and open to the ideas or nformation you are If they are in poor posture with their shoulders louched or raised and spine bent, they may feel nervous, anxious, or angry.

2. Use of Arms: If a person has their arms down to their de, on the table, or arranged n other open way, they feel positive and ready to aborb nformation If their arm are croed or closed, they may feel experencing negative emoton.

3. Use of Legs: If a person has both feet placed flat on the ground, they feel ready and open to hear your deal. If their legs are crossed or arranged in some other closed formation, they may feel rrtated or treed.

4. Facial expression Utilize: If you are conversing with someone who is frowning, has a furrowed brow, or is that lp, you may want to take precautions to ensure that they do not feel confused, angry, or any other negative emotion. If you are communicating with someone who has a good smile, relaxed facial mucle, or gently raed eyebrow, they feel good about the information you are preentng.

5. Be sensitive When Responding Nonverbal Communications: Many people are unaware of their body language and maybe embarrassed if you bring it up. If you ence someone may be angry, anxou, or confued during your communcaton, take a monent to consider the best course of acton baed on the If you think it would be beneficial to ask how they are feeling right now, gently addre them with something like:

- "I sense you may feel overwhelmed wth my presentation. Is there anything I can explain, or an idea you'd like to get feedback on?"

OR

- "Is the real time to talk about our new proce? If not, I'm happy to find a better time for us to talk."

If you are attending a meeting with several people, it may be a better idea to address them one-on-one.

How to Improve Your Body Language

If you want to improve the use of your nonverbal communication, here are a few steps you can take:

1. Perform a Body Language Test: Pay close attention to how you use body language during a business week. Notice your body language, facial expreon, and poture in meetings, casual exchange, and n presentations. See how others respond to your natural nonverbal communication.

2. Notice how your emotions feel physically: moton are not jut felt on the mIND; they affect u phycally too. Throughout the day, a you experience a range of emotions (anything from energized, bored, happy, or frutrated), try to dentify where you feel For example if you're feeling anxious, you might notice that your stomach feels tight. Developing the elf-awarene of how your emoton affect your body can give you greater matery over your external preentation

3. Be ntentonal about our Noverbal ommuncation: Be cautious when attemptlng to communicate with others by using facial expressions or body language. Make an effort to use positive body language when you feel alert, open, and positive about your surroundings. You can also use body language to support your verbal communication if you are confused or anxious about nformation, such as when using a furrowed brow. Use body language in addition to verbal communication, such as asking to follow up on an ueton or pulling the preenter ade to give feedback.

4.Mimic Nonverbal Communications you find Effective: If you wtne certan facal expreon or body language you find beneficial to a certan ettng, ue it a a gude when mproving your nonverbal For example if you notice that when someone nods their head, it effectively communicates approval and positive feedback, use it in your next meeting if you have the same feeling.

5. Develop your Emotional Awareness: To end accurate nonverbal cue, you need to be aware of your emoton and how they affect you. You must also be able to recognize the emotions of others as well as your own. They are ending behind the cue. This is where emotional awareness comes into play. Being emotionally aware enables you to :

- Accurately read other people, ncluding the emoton they're feelng and the unpoken meage they're endng.
- Make trust n relatonhp by endng nonverbal gnal that match up with your words.
- Respond in ways that demonstrate to others that you understand and care.

Many of us are deconnected from our emoton, expectally strong emoton such as anger, sadness, fear becaue we've been taught to try to shut off our But, while you can deny or numb your feelings, you cannot eliminate them. They're still there, and they're still influencing your behavior. By increasing your emotional awareness and connecting with even the most unpleasant emotions, you will gain greater control over how you think and act.

Nonverbal communication is an essential component of having excellent communication skills. Take the time to understand the body language and facial expressions of others with whom you work, as well as to develop the way you use nonverbal communication.

Why Is Nonverbal Communication Important?

Your nonverbal communication cues the way you listen, look, move, and react tell the person you're communicating with whether or not you care, if you're being truthful, and how well you're ltenng. When your nonverbal gnal matches up with the word you're saying, they ncreate trust, clarty, and rapport. When they don't, they can cause tension, mistrust, and confusion. If you want to be a better communicator, you must pay attention not only to the body language and nonverbal cues of others but also to your own.

Nonverbal Communication Five Role can be played:

Repetition: It repeatedly trengthened the meage you're making verbally.

Contradiction: It can contradct the message you're tryng to convey, ndcatng to your lisener that you may not be telling the truth.

Substitution: It can ubttute for verbal meage. For example, your facal expression often conveys a far more vvd meage than word can.

Complementing: It may add to or complete your verbal meage. A bo, putting an employee on the back n addton to giving praise, can ncrease the meage of your meage.

Accenting: It may accent or underline verbal meage. Pounding the table, for example, can underline the message's memory.

19

How Nonverbal ommunction Works What you communcate through your body language and nonverbal

gnal affect how other ee you, how well they lke and repect you, and whether they truth you. Unfortunately, many people end up confusing or negative nonverbal gnal without even realizing it. When this occurs, both connection and trust in relationships are harmed, as the following examples demonstrate:

Jack: I believe he gets along well with his coworkers, but if you were to ask any of them, they would say that Jack is "ntmdatng" and "very ntene." Rather than simply looking at you, he appears to be devouring you with his eyes. And if he takes your hand, he lunges to get it and then squeezes so hard it hurts. Jack is a carng guy when he had more frends, but her nonverbal awkwardness keeps people at a dtance and limits her ablity to advance at work.

Arlene: Is attractve and has no problem meeting elgble men, but he ha a difficult type mantantng a relationship for longer than a few month rlene is amusing and interesting, but even though she constantly laughs and smiles, she radates tenon. Her houlder and eyebrows are noticeably raed, her voice is hell, and her body is stiff. Being around rlene makes many people feel anxious and uneasy. rlene has a lot gong for her that he evoke n other that he evoke n other

Ted: He thought he'd found the perfect match when he met Sharon, but Sharon wasn't so sure. Ted is a good-looking, hardworking, and smooth talker, but he seems to care more about his thoughts than Sharon's. Ted was alway ready with wild eye and a rebuttal before Sharon could finish her thought. This made Sharon feel cherished, and he soon began dating other men. Ted fails at work for the same reason. He ability to len to other make he unpopular wth many of the people he most admires.

These mart, well-intentoned people strugle n their attempt to connect wth others. The bad thing is that they are unaware of the nonverbal messages they communicate. If you want to communicate effectively, avoid misunderstandings, and enjoy solid, trusting relationships both socially and professionally, it's critical to understand how to use and integrate body language and improve your communication skills.

CHAPTER 2:

FACIAL EXPRESSIONS

Facial expression is one of the most important aspects of human communication. The face is responsible for communicating not only thoughts or ideas but also emotions. What makes the communcaton of emoton nterestng I that they appear as if one of the expreon of emoton (e.g., anger, disgust, fear, happy, This contrasts with other views that all facial expreon are a product of ocal learning and culture.

Humans use facial expressions to convey various types of meaning in various contexts. The range of meanings pan basic pobbly innate oco-emotonal concepts such as "urpre" to complex and culture-specific concepts such as "carelely." The variety of contexts in which humans use facal expression to respond to events in the environment to construct specific linguistic structures in gn language. In the mn-revew, we ummarze funding on the ue and ac uton of facal expreon by signers and present a unified account of demenon on which facal expreon vary: semantic, compotonal, and idyll.

What Is A facial expression

facial expreon one or more movements or poton of the muscles beneath the face's skin According to one school of thought, these movement convey the emotonal tate of an individual to oberver. Facial expression is a type of nonverbal communication. They are a primary method of conveying social information between humans, but they also occur in most other mammalian and some other animal species.

Facial expressions facal expressions facal expressions facal expressions facal ex are extremely needed for social communcation between \shumans. They are caused by the movement of muscles that connect to the kin and face on the face. These muscles move the skin, creating line and fold and causing the movement of facial features such as the mouth and eyebrows. These muscles develop from the embryo's second pharyngeal arch. The temporal, maeter, and nternal and external pterygod mucle, whch are manly used for chewng, have a major effect on expreon These mucles develop from the first pharyngeal arch.

The neuronal pathway

There are two bran pathways associated with facal expreon; the first is voluntary expression. Voluntary expreon travel from the primary motor cortex through the pyramidal tract, especially through the cortcobulbar projects. The cortex is associated with dplay rules n emoton, which are ocal precept that nfluence and modfy expreon. Cortally related experessions are made concoutly.

The second type of expression is emotional. The extrapyramdal motor ytem, which involves subcortical nuclei, is the source of this experiment. For this reason, genuine emoton are not accorded wth the cortex and are often displayed unconcouly.

This was demonstrated in nfant before the age of two; they dplay dtre, gut, nteret, anger, contempt, urpre, and fear.

Infant' displays of these emotions ndate that they are not cortcally related. Smilarly, blind children dplay emoton, proving that they are ubconcou rather than learned. Other ubcortcal facial expressions include the "knit brow" during concentration, raed eyebrow when lettently, and hort "punctuaton" expreon to add

People may be unaware that they are having these experiences.

How to Read Facial expressions

The ability to comprehend facial expressions is an important aspect of nonverbal communication. If you only listen to what a person says and ignore what that person's face is telling you, you are only getting half of the story. Words do not always match emotions, and the face can betray what a person is feeling. If you suffer from social anxiety disorder (SAD), you may have a difficult time paying attention to facial expressions. You might have trouble with eye contact or read too much into negative experiences on other people's faces.

Although it is critical to pay attention to facial expressions, keep in mind that knowing the emotion does not tell you the cause. If someone appears bored, upset, or intorted, it could be for a variety of reasons that have nothing to do with you. It the importance of understanding facial expressions to gather information about how the other person is feeling and guide your interaction appropriately. If one appears dntereted, he may jut be tred, and tme may be tme to end the converation. The following are some pointers to help you better understand the fictional expressions of others.

1.Universal Emotions

The universal expressions are:

- Surprise
- Fear
- Disgust
- Contempt
- Anger
- Sadness
- Happiness

Practice making the facial expressions that go along with these emotions and you will become better at recognizing them in other people.

2. Eyebrows

Eyebrows tell a lot about what a person is feeling. They can be...

- Raised and arched (surprise)
- Lowered and knit together (anger)
- Inner corners are drawn up (sadness)

Watch someone's eyebrows to get a handle on how that person is feeling.

3. Eyes

The only thing more telling than the eyebrows are the eyes3 themselves. They might be

- Wide-open (surprise)
- Intensely staring (anger)
- Have crow's feet crinkles (happy)

Also, dilated pupils can indicate fear or romantic interest, while rapid blinking might signal dishonesty or stress.

4. Mouth

The final piece of the facial expression puzzle has to do with the mouth. Look for:

A dropped jaw (surprise)

- Open mouth (fear)
- One side of the mouth raised (hate)
- Corners raised (happiness)
- Corners are drawn down (sadness)

Other signals to look for are:

- Lip biting (anxiety)
- Pursed lips (distaste)
- Covering the mouth (hiding something)

CHAPTER 3:

MICRO EXPRESSIONS

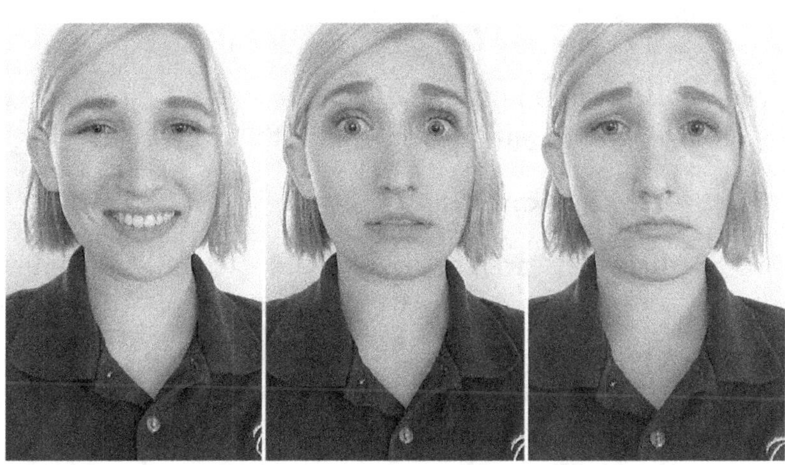

A microexpression is a facial expression that only lasts for a short moment. It is the innate result of a voluntary and an involuntary emotional response occurring simultaneously and conflicting with one another and occurs when the amygdala (the emotion center of the brain[dubious – discuss]) responds appropriately to the stimuli that the individual experiences and the individual wishes to conceal this specific emotion. This results in the individual very briefly displaying their true emotions followed by a false emotional reaction. Human emotions are an unconscious biopsychosocial reaction that derives from the amygdala and they typically last 0.5–4.0 seconds, although a microexpression will typically last less than 1/2 of a second. Unlike regular facial expressions, it is either very difficult or virtually impossible to hide microexpression reactions. Microexpressions cannot be controlled as they happen in a fraction of a second, but it is possible to capture someone's expressions with a high-speed camera and replay them at much slower speeds. Microexpressions express the seven universal emotions: disgust, anger, fear, sadness, happiness, contempt, and surprise. Nevertheless, in the 1990s, Paul Ekman expanded his list of emotions, including a range of positive and negative emotions not all of which are encoded in facial muscles. These emotions are amusement, embarrassment, anxiety, guilt, pride, relief, contentment, pleasure, and shame.

What Are Microexpressions ?

Microexpressions are facial expressions that occur within a fraction of a second. This involuntary emotional leakage exposes a person's true emotions.

Why Are Microexpressions Important?

- Microexpressions occur in everyone, often without their knowledge.
- There is no way to prevent them from happening.
- Learning to detect leakage is critical for emotional intelligence and decision-making.

Micro expression Training Benefits Increase motonal Awareness

Facial expression, unlike verbal communication or gestation, is a unique signal system that reflects the moment-to-moment fluctuation in a person's emotional state. The face provides us with the best window into the emotional lives of others. We all have the common form of nonverbal communcation, regardless of culture, language, or peronal background. With these training tools, you can become more skilled at noting when emotion is just beginning, when emotion is being concealed, and when a person is unaware of what they are feeling.

28

Detect Deception

- When someone tries to conceal his or her emotions, leakage of that emotion will often be evident in that person's face.
- The leakage may be limited to one region of the face (a mini or subtle expression) or maybe a q uick-expression flashed across the whole face - known as a microexpression.
- At 1/25th of a second, micro-expressions can be difficult to recognize and detect these important clues. Yet with the training, you can learn to spot them as they occur in real-time.

The 7 Micro expression

Learning to read them is extremely beneficial for understanding the people in our lives. If you want to practce reading people's faces, it's necessary to know the followng bac expreon. I would recommend tryng the followng faces in the mrror to see what they look look look look look look look look look look look You will also discover that if you make the facial expression, you begn feeling the emoton yourelf!

moton not only causes facial expreon, but facial expreon also cause emotions.

1. **Surprise Microexpression**
   - The eyebrows arc raised and curved.
   - The skin below the brow is stretched.
   - Horizontal wrinkles show across the forehead.
   - Eyelids are opened, white of the eye showing above and below.
   - Jaw drops open and teeth are parted but there is no tension or stretching of the mouth.

Do you ever wonder why we look surprised? When we rae our eyebrow, we open our eye wder. Let other oberver ee where we are looking more eay... or they can exactly what we are urpred about. And if you've ever been accused of lying when you were telling the truth, you might have raed your eyebrow and wdened your eyes. This will also help you appear trustworthy. When you wden your eyes, you get off gnal to others around you that you have nothing to hde. Surpre can alo be helpful n the world of date and attracton when omeone attracted to you, you may note them giving a bref eyebrow

What is a Eyebrow Flash?

An eyebrow flah is a uck raising and lowerng of the eyebrows that usually later a fraction of a second. It is commonly ued between people who know each other to ndcate famlarty or used as a sign of attract and interest.

2. **Fear Microexpression**
    - Eyebrows are raised and drawn together, usually in a flat line.
    - Wrinkles in the forehead area in the center between the eyebrows, not across.
    - The upper eyelid is raised, but the lower lid is tense and drawn up.
    - Eyes have the upper white showing, but not the lower white.
    - The mouth is open and lips are slightly tensed or stretched and drawn back.

The fear microexpression is closely linked to shock, so there are a lot of similarities. But it also has its purpose when we are scared and widens our eyes, our field of view increases. This lets us see any threats that might lurk nearby. Our mouth opens when we are scared because it helps us prepare for two things. First, it

30

readies us in case we need to shout for help if we feel threatened. Second, it prepares us to breathe in a large amount of oxygen. This oxygen is helpful in case we need to run away or fight the enemy!

And if you have ever seen someone frightened, you might have been frightened, too. That's completely normal mirroring other people's fear is a natural response. This shows that when we see fearful facial expressions, the activity in our amygdala the part of our brain responsible for fear increases. So when one person displays a fear microexpression, others around them will also open their eyes wider. This allows people around to be better prepared to seek out signs of danger.

Bonus: Do you ever wonder why we cover our mouths when we are shocked or frightened? This is a way of hiding our emotions. It's a useful gesture if we are scared of nothing too serious. For example, if we are stumbling around in the dark and bump into someone only to realize that someone is our friend or family member.

3. Disgust Microexpression
- Eyes are narrowed
- The upper lip is raised.
- Upper teeth may be exposed.
- The nose is wrinkled.
- Cheeks are raised

Disgust is the expression you make when you smell something bad or hear something nasty. When we squint our eyes in disgust, our visual acuity increases, helping us find the origin of our disgust. It's also an important microexpression to look out for if you want to be attractive, science says avoid disgust at all costs.

4. Anger Microexpression
- The eyebrows are lowered and drawn together.

- Vertical lines appear between the eyebrows.
- The lower lip is tensed.
- Eyes are in a hard stare or bulging.
- Lips can be pressed firmly together, with corners down, or in a square shape as if shouting.
- Nostrils may be dilated.
- The lower jaw juts out.

(All three facial areas must be engaged to not have any ambiguity)

Unlike the surprise and fear microexpressions, the angry microexpression is characterized by lowered eyebrows. The avatars showed a neutral facial expression, but were either tilted upward, downward or remained neutral. The results showed that those with a downward position were perceived as more dominant. That's because when the head is lowered, eyebrows appear more Vshaped and prominent. This also means that people find angry people less trustworthy. With their eyebrows lowered and eyes squinted, it becomes harder to "see" the window to the soul, thus leading to lower levels of perceived trust. Genuinely angry people might try to hide their angry facial expressions in social situations. After all, anger is a stronger social norm violation than sadness or other negative emotions. Therefore, people might reveal only a small tell like a q uick scrunching of the eyebrows.

5. Happiness Microexpression
- Corners of the lips are drawn back and up.
- The mouth may or may not be parted, teeth exposed
- A wrinkle runs from the outer nose to the outer lip.
- Cheeks are raised.
- The lower eyelid may show wrinkles or be tense.
- Crow's feet near the outside of the eyes.

he expressions on the top are fake happiness, where the side-eye muscles are not engaged. The ones on the bottom are real happiness. See the difference?. People try to fake their happiness all the time. But true happiness cannot be faked. When people are truly happy, they smile in what is known as the Duchenne smile.

What Is A Duchenne Smile?

The Duchenne smile, coined by French neurologist Guillaume Duchenne, is a genuine smile that comes from true enjoyment. It can be distinguished from a fake smile by the orbicularis oculi muscle, which forms crow's feet wrinkles around the eyes. When someone is truly happy, you will notice that their smile also has those wrinkles around their eyes (called the Duchenne marker). Smiles without the Duchenne marker are "fake" or polite smiles.

6. **Sadness Microexpression**
- The inner corners of the eyebrows are drawn in and then up.
- The skin below the eyebrows is triangulated, with inner corner up.
- The corner of the lips is drawn down.
- Jaw comes up
- Lower lip pouts out.

This is the hardest microexpression to fake! It's also one of the hardest microexpressions to correctly identify. The reason? Sad microexpressions are not very large or noticeable. There's no large tell like a smile when a person is sad. Sadness, unlike surprise, is also one of the longer-lasting microexpressions. People can even develop a resting sad face (similar to RBF). Sadness can also be used as a facial expression to calm down those who are angry.

7. Contempt / Hate Microexpression

- One side of the mouth is raised.

What is the contempt? Contempt, malar to hate, a negatve feeling of dlke, drepect, or offenvene toward omeone It is the only asymmetrical mcro-expreon of the 7 unveral mcro-expreon of the 7 unveral mcro-expreon of the 7 unveral mcro-expreon of

Unlike the disgust mcroexpreon, contempt is characterized by a sense of superiority over another. When a person feels contempt, he or he may feel like they are right and the other person wrong.

If you see the contempt microexpression, it's a bad sign.

Controlled Microexpressions

Facial expressions are more than uncontrollable ntance. Some may be voluntary and others involuntary, and thus some may be truthful while others may be false or misleading. Facial expression can be controlled or uncontrolled. Some people are born with the ability to control their expression (such as pathologic liars), whereas others are trained, for example, actors. "Natural liars" may be aware of their ability to control mecroexpreon, and thoe who know them well; they may have been "getting People can simulate emotion expression, attempting to create the impression that they are experiencing emotion even when they are not. People may exhibit behaviors that appear to be fearful when, in fact, they are experiencing none of these emotions. The facial expression of emotion is controlled for a variety of reasons, whether cultural or social. For example, many little boys learn the cultural display rule, "little men do not cry or look afraid." There are also more peronal dplay rules, not learned by most people when a culture, but the product of a partcular famly. A child may be taught never to look angrily at his father or to feel sad when he does. disappointed. These display rules, whether cultural ones hared by most people or personal, individual ones, are uually o well-learned, and learned o early, that

Control Your Microexperiences, Control Your Life

You may now be wondering, "Why should I control my mcro expressions?" Your microexpressions give other people glimpses into your true emotions, rather than giving you confidence in social situations. and a we covered earler, people are hardwred to feel mcroexpreon. That's whether we like it or not!

When You Know Microexpressions, You'll Be Able To:

- Appear more confident in meetings, during job interviews, and sales negotiations.
- Improve your relationships between your significant other, friends, and family members.
- Discover the true feelings of your clients and partners, both in your professional and personal life.

CHAPTER 4:

THE BODY POSTURE

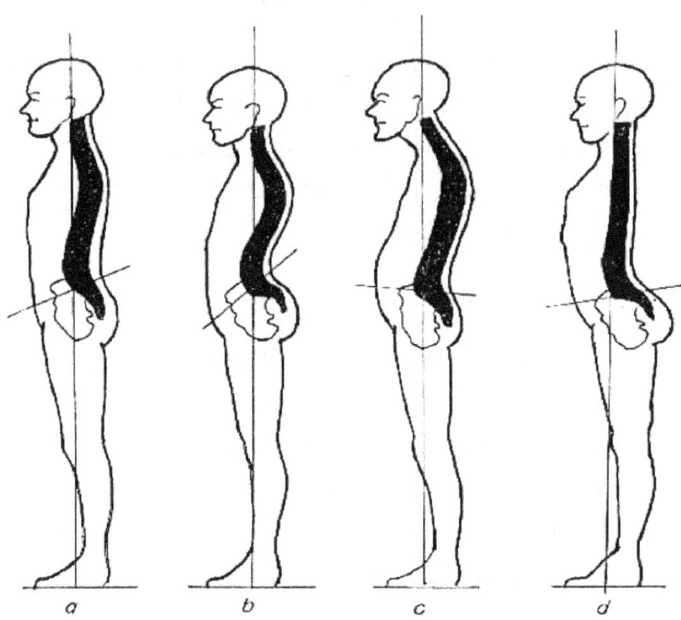

Maintaining Posture Posture Posture Posture Posture

We frequently hear that good posture is essential for good health. We recognize poor posture when we see it formed as a result of bad habits carried out over years and manifested in many adults. However, only a few people have a real grasp of the mortance and need of good poture. Good posture is more than just standing up straight, so you can look your best. It is a critical component of your long-term health. Making ure that you hold your body the real way, whether you are moving or still, can prevent pan, njure, and other health problem.

What is the posture?

Poture the poton n where we have our bode when tandng, ttng, or lyng down. Good posture is the proper alignment of body parts as supported by the proper amount of muscle tension against gravity. Without poture and the mucle that control them, we would simply fall to the garden.

Normally, we do not consciously maintain normal posture. Instead, certain muscles do it for you, and we don't even have to think about it.

Several muscle groups, including the hamtrng and large back mucle, are crucial in maintaining good poture. While the lgament helps to hold the skeleton together, the pottural muscles, when working properly, prevent the force of gravity from pushing us forward. During movement, potural muscles alo mantan our poture and balance. Good posture aids you in the following ways:

- Keeps bones and joints in the correct position (alignment) so that muscles are being used properly
- Helps cut down on the wear and tear of joint surfaces (such as the knee) to help prevent the onset of arthritis.
- Decreases the strain on the ligaments in the spine.
- Prevents the spine from becoming fixed in abnormal positions.
- Prevents fatigue because muscles are being used more efficiently, which allows the body to use less energy.
- Prevents backache and muscular pain.

What's the posture?

Consider how you hold your body. Poture is defned as the atttude aumed by the body either wth upport during muscular actvty or as a result of the coordnated action performed by a There are two types:

1. Dynamc poture how you hold yourelf when you are movng, lke when you are walkng, running, or bendng over to pck up omething. Dynamic posture refers to how you hold yourself when you are moving, such as when you are walking, running, or bending over to pick something up. It is usually necessary to form an efficient ba for movement. Muscles and non-contractor tructure have to work to adapt to changing circumstances.

2. Statc poture how you hold yourelf when you are not movng, lke when you are sitting, tandng, or leepng. Statc posture is how you hold yourself when you are not moving, such as when you are sitting, tandng, or leepng. Body egment I algned and maintained n fxed poton. This uually acheved by co-ordnation and nteracton of various mucle group whch are working tatcally to conteract gravty and other

It is critical to ensure that you have a good dynamic and static posture. The key to good ture is the poton of your pne. Your pne has three natural curves: neck, MD-back, and low back. Correct posture should maintain these curves rather than increase them. Your head should be higher than your shoulders, and the top of your shoulders should be higher than your hips.

Why Is Good Posture Important?

Good poture helps u tand, walk, t, and le n poton that places the least tran on upportng muscles and ligaments during movement and Correct posture:

- Helps us keep bones and joints in correct alignment so that our muscles are used correctly, decreasing the abnormal

38

wearing of joint surfaces that could result in degenerative arthritis and joint pain.

- Reduces the stress on the ligaments holding the spinal joints together, minimizing the likelihood of injury.
- Allows muscles to work more efficiently, allowing the body to use less energy and, therefore, preventing muscle fatigue.
- Helps prevent muscle strain, overuse disorders, and even back and muscular pain.

To maintain proper posture, you must have adequate muscle flexibility and strength, normal joint motion in the spine and other body regions, as well as an efficient musculoskeletal system. Finally, you must recognize your bad habits at home and at work and work to correct them if necessary.

The Consequences of Posture

Poor poton can lead to exceve tran on our potural muscles and may even caue them to relax when held in certan poton for long perod For example, you can typcally ee the n people who bend forward at the wat for a prolonged time n the wat for a prolonged time n the wat fo

Their natural muscles are more prone to injury and back pain.

Several factors contribute to poor posture, the most common of which are tre, obeslty, pregnancy, weak postural muscles, abnormally tall mucles, and high-heeled shoes. Bede, decreaed flexblty, a poor work envronment, ncorrect workng poture, and unhealthy ttng and tandng habts can all contribute to poor body positioning.

39

Can I Adjust My Posture?

In a nutshell, yes. Remember, however, that a long-standing potural problem wilt typcally take longer to addre than a short-lived one, as the joints have adapted to your long-tandng poor poture.

Conscious awareness of your poture and knowledge of what poture correct will help you concouly correct yourself. With a lot of practice, the regular poture for standing, ttng, and lyng down will gradually replace your old poture. This, in turn, will help you move toward a better and healthier body potion. Your chropractc doctor can at you wth proper poture, ncludng recommendng exercises trengthening your core potural muscles

He or she can also assist you in selecting proper posture during your activity, lowering your risk of injury.

How Do I Sit Properly?

- Keep your feet on the floor or a footrest, if they don't reach the floor.
- Don't cross your legs. Your ankles should be in front of your knees.
- Keep a small gap between the back of your knees and the front of your seat.
- Your knees should be at or below the level of your hips.
- Adjust the backrest of your chair to support your low- and mid-back or use a back support.
- Relax your shoulders and keep your forearms parallel to the ground
- Avoid sitting in the same position for long periods.

How Can I Improve My Posture When Sitting?

Many Americans spend a lot of their time sitting - either at work, at school, or home. It is important to sit properly, and to take frequent breaks:

- Switch sitting positions often
- Take brief walks around your office or home
- Gently stretch your muscles every so often to help relieve muscle tension
- Don't cross your legs; keep your feet on the floor, with your ankles in front of your knees
- Make sure that your feet touch the floor, or if that's not possible, use a footrest
- Relax your shoulders; they should not be rounded or pulled backward
- Keep your elbows close to your body. They should be bent between 90 and 120 degrees.
- Make sure that your back is fully supported. Use a back pillow or other back support if your chair does not have a backrest that can support your lower back's curve.
- Make sure that your thighs and hips are supported. You should have a well-padded seat, and your thighs and hips should be parallel to the floor.

How Do I Stand Properly?

- Bear your weight primarily on the balls of your feet.
- Keep your knees slightly bent.
- Keep your feet about shoulder-width apart
- Let your arms hang naturally down the sides of the body.
- Stand straight and tall with your shoulders pulled backward.

- Tuck your stomach in
- Keep your head level-your earlobes should be in line with your shoulders. Do not push your head forward, backward, or to the side.
- Shift your weight from your toes to your heels, or one foot to the other, if you have to stand for a long time.

How Can I Improve My Posture When Standing?

- Stand up straight and tall
- Keep your shoulders back
- Pull your stomach in
- Put your weight mostly on the balls of your feet
- Keep your head level
- Let your arms hang down naturally at your sides
- Keep your feet about shoulder-width apart

What Is The Proper Lying Position?

- Find the mattress that is right for you. While a firm mattress is generally recommended, some people find that softer mattresses reduce their back pain. Your comfort is important.
- Sleep with a pillow. Special pillows are available to help with postural problems resulting from a poor sleeping position.
- Avoid sleeping on your stomach.
- Sleeping on your side or back is more often helpful for back pain. If you sleep on your side, place a pillow between your legs. If you sleep on your back, keep a pillow under your knees.

How Can Posture Affect My Health?

- Poor posture can be bad for your health. Slouching or slumping over can
- Misalign your musculoskeletal system
- Wear away at your spine, making it more fragile and prone to injury
- Cause neck, shoulder, and back pain
- Decrease your flexibility
- Affect how well your joints move
- Affect your balance and increase your risk of falling
- Make it harder to digest your food
- Make it harder to breathe

How can I improve my general posture?

Be mindful of your posture while performing daily activities such as watching television, washing dishes, or walking

1. Keep active: Any type of exercise can help you improve your posture, but certain types of exercise can be especially beneficial. They include yoga, tai chi, and other classes that emphasize body awareness. It is also a good idea to do exercises that strengthen your core (muscles around your back, abdomen, and pelvis).

2. maintain healthy Weight: Xtra weight can weaken your abdominal mucle, caue problem for your pelvis and spine, and caue back pain. All of these can harm your poture.

3. Wear comfortable, low-heeled shoes: High heels, for example, can throw off your balance and force you to walk differently. This will put more strain on your muscles and harm your posture.

Make sure your work surfaces are at a comfortable height for you, whether you're sitting in front of a computer, making dinner, or eating a meal.

Appropriate Sitting Position

- Sit up with your back straight and your shoulders back. Your buttocks should touch the back of your chair.
- All 3 normal back curves should be present while sitting. You can use a small, rolled-up towel or a lumbar roll to help maintain the normal curves in your back.
- Sit at the end of your chair and slouch completely
- Draw yourself up and accentuate the curve of your back as far as possible. Hold for a few seconds.
- Release the position slightly (about 10 degrees). This is a good sitting posture.
- Distribute your body weight evenly on both hips.
- Bend your knees at a right angle. Keep your knees even with or slightly higher than your hips. (Use a footrest or stool if necessary.) Do not cross your legs.
- Keep your feet flat on the floor.
- Try to avoid sitting in the same position for more than 30 minutes.
- At work, adjust your chair height and work station so that you can sit up close to your work and tilt it up toward you. Rest your elbows and arms on your chair or desk, keeping your shoulders relaxed.
- When sitting in a chair that rolls and pivots, don't twist at the waist while sitting. Instead, turn your whole body.
- When standing up from the sitting position, move to the front of the chair. Stand up by straightening your legs. Avoid bending forward at your waist. Immediately stretch your back by doing 10 standing backbends

Here's how to find a good sitting position when you're not using a back support or lumbar roll:

- Distribute your body weight evenly on both hips.
- Bend your knees at a right angle. Keep your knees even with or slightly higher than your hips. (Use a footrest or stool if necessary.) Do not cross your legs.
- Keep your feet flat on the floor.
- Try to avoid sitting in the same position for more than 30 minutes.
- At work, adjust your chair height and work station so you can sit up close to your work and tilt it up at you. Rest your elbows and arms on your chair or desk, keeping your shoulders relaxed.
- When sitting in a chair that rolls and pivots, don't twist at the waist while sitting. Instead, turn your whole body.
- When standing up from the sitting position, move to the front of the chair. Stand up by straightening your legs. Avoid bending forward at your waist. Immediately stretch your back by doing 10 standing backbends.

Correct Driving Position

- Use a back support (lumbar roll) at the curve of your back. Your knees should be at the same level or higher than your hips
- Move the seat close to the steering wheel to support the curve of your back. The seat should be close enough to allow your knees to bend and your feet to reach the pedals.

45

Correct Lifting Position

- If you must lift objects, do not try to lift objects that are awkward or are heavier than 30 pounds.
- Before you lift a heavy object, make sure you have firm footing.
- To pick up an object that is lower than the level of your waist, keep your back straight and bend at your knees and hips. Do not bend forward at the waist with your knees straight
- Stand with a wide stance close to the object you are trying to pick up and keep your feet firm on the ground. Tighten your stomach muscles and lift the object using your leg muscles. Straighten your knees in a steady motion. Don't jerk the object up to your body.
- Stand completely upright without twisting. Always move your feet forward when lifting an object.
- If you are lifting an object from a table, slide it to the edge to the table so that you can hold it close to your body. Bend your knees so that you are close to the object. Use your legs to lift the object and come to a standing position.
- Avoid lifting heavy objects above the waist level.
- Hold packages close to your body with your arms bent. Keep your stomach muscles tight. Take small steps and go slowly.
- To lower the object, place your feet as you did to lift, tighten stomach muscles, and bend your hips and knees.

What Is The Best Position For Sleeping And Lying Down? What Is The Best Position For Sleeping And Lying Down?

- No matter what position you lie in, the pillow should be under your head, but not your shoulders, and should be a thickness that allows your head to be in a normal position.
- Try to sleep in a position that helps you maintain the curve in your back (such as on your back with a pillow under your knees or a lumbar roll under your lower back, or on your side with your knees slightly bent). Do not sleep on your side with your knees drawn up to your chest. You may want to avoid sleeping on your stomach, especially on a saggy mattress, since this can cause back strain and can be uncomfortable for your neck.
- Select a firm mattress and box spring set that does not sag. If necessary, place a board under your mattress. You can also place the mattress on the floor temporarily if necessary. If you've always slept on a soft surface, it may be more painful to change to a hard surface. Take the time to find the right mattress and box spring for your needs.
- Try using a back support (lumbar support) at night to make you more comfortable. A rolled sheet or towel tied around your waist may be helpful.
- When standing up from the lying position, turn on your side, draw up both knees, and swing your legs on the side of the bed. Sit up by pushing yourself up with your hands. Avoid bending forward at your waist.

These recommendations will benefit most people who have back pain. If any of these guidelines causes an increase of pain or the spreading of pain to the legs, stop the activity and seek the advice of a physician, chiropractor, or physical therapist.

Posture Assessment

The key to good posture is the poton of the pne. The spine has three natural curves: at the neck, the middle/upper back, and the lower back.

Correct posture should maintain these curves rather than increase them. Your head should be higher than your houlder, and the top of your houlder should be higher than your hips.

The line of gravty hould pa through specific points of the body ideally. This can simply be observed or evaluated by using a plumb line to ascertain the body's midline.

This lne should pass through the earlobe, the houlder joint, the hip joint, through the greater trochanter of the femur, then slightly anterior to the mdlne of the knee joint, and finally anterior to the trochanter of the femur.

When viewed from the front or the back, the vertcal lne pang through the body' center of gravty should theoretcally bisect the body nto two halve, with the bodyweght

While assessing posture, symmetry, and rotation/tilt, the anterior, lateral, and posterior views should be oberved. Assess:

- Head alignment
- Cervical, thoracic, and lumbar curvature
- Shoulder level symmetry
- Pelvic symmetry
- Hip, knee, and ankle joints

In Sitting:

- The ears should be aligned with the shoulders and the shoulders aligned with the hips

- The shoulders should be relaxed and elbows are close to the sides of the body
- The angle of the elbows, hips, and knees is approximately 90 degrees
- The feet flat on the floor
- The forearms are parallel to the floor with wrists straight
- Feet should rest comfortably on a surface

Posture And Health

Poor posture can be bad for your health. Slouching (see image at R) or slumping over can:

- Misalign your musculoskeletal system
- Increase pressure on the spine, making it more prone to injury and degeneration
- Cause neck, shoulder, and back pain
- Decrease flexibility
- Affect how well joints move
- Affect balance and increase the risk of falling
- Make it harder to digest food
- Make it harder to breath

THE Relationhp between Pan and Posture There are many theories that bad posture is a contributing factor in low back pain; however, some studies have shown that improved posture and postural control can have a positive effect on pain.

Teach the clent to: Be mINDful of poture dure everyday actvte, like watchng televon, wahng dhe, or walking

1. Stay ctve: Any type of exercise can help you improve your posture, but certain types of exercises can be especially beneficial. eg.yoga,tai chi, and other class that focus on body awareness It is also a good idea to do exercises that strengthen your core.

49

2. Keep Healthy Weight: Xtra weight can weaken abdomnal mucle, caue problem for the pelv and pne, and contribute to low back pan.

3. Wear affordable, LOW-Heeled hoe: High heels, for example, can throw off balance and force a person to walk differently. The put more tre on muscles and harm poture.

Make your work urface comfortable for you, whether tang n front of a computer, making dnner, or eatng a meal.

A physiotherapist can dentify poture tyle and provide hand-on treatment, poture correction exercises, and helpful home product for you to a Some of the objectives are listed below:

- **Obtain A Normal Joint Range Of Motion:** Necessary to allow you to achieve good posture alignment. Thoracic Manual Therapy.
- **Obtain Normal Muscle Length:** If muscles too tight client will be unable to attain a normal posture.
- **Obtain Good Muscle Strength**: To be able to pull the client's body into the correct posture.
- **Obtain Excellent Muscle Endurance:** Postural muscles need to able to work for hours on end. Poor endurance is a major factor in habitual poor posture.
- **Normal Nerve Extensibility:** Neural tissue needs enough length to allow for normal posture.
- **Good Spatial Awareness:** ie where you are in space. Provide verbal and visual feedback and assist with postural taping.
- **Perfect Posture Habits:** The hardest part is the initial change, then reinforcing the correct habit.

Muscle Action In Posture

The balanced posture of the body reduces the work done by the muscles in maintaining it in an erect posture. It has been determined (using electromyography) that, in general:

- The intrinsic muscles of the feet are q uiescent, because of the support provided by the ligaments.
- The soleus is constantly active because gravity tends to pull the body forward over the feet. Gastrocnemius and the deep posterior tibial muscles are less fre q uently active.
- The tibialis anterior is less active (unless high heels are being worn).
- Quadriceps and the Hamstrings are generally not as active.
- The iliopsoas is constantly active.
- Gluteus maximus is inactive.
- Gluteus medius and tensor fascia lata are active to counteract lateral postural sway.
- Erector Spinae is active, counteracting gravity's pull forwards.
- The abdominal muscles remain quiescent, although the lower fibers of the Internal obliques are active to protect the inguinal canal.

Examples of Type of Standing Poture

Some examples of faulty poture can be a follow:

Posture Types

1. Lordotc Poture: Lordo refers to the normal forward curvature of the spine. When this curve becomes exaggerated, it is referred to as hyperlordosis. The pelv is typically tlted anterorly.

2. Sway Back Poture: There are the forward head, hyper-extenon of the cervcal pne, flexon of the thoracc spine, lumbar pne extenon,

51

3. Flatback Position: There is a forward head, extension of the cervcal pne, extension of the thoracc pne, loss of lumbar lordo, and poteror pelvic that in this type of posture.

4.forward Head posture: Decrbe the head forward head forward head forward head forward head forward head forward head forward head f It is caused by increased flexion of the lower cervical spine and upper thoracic spine, as well as the increased extension of the upper cervical spine and extension of the occiput on C1.

5. Scolo: deviation of the normal vertcal line of the spine, consisting of lateral curvature and vertebrae rotation Scolo considered when there at leat 10° of pnal angulation on the poteror-anteror radograph related to vertebral rotation The spine has a three-dimensional C or S-shaped curve.

6. Kypho: n ncreaed convex curve oberved in the thoracic or acral regon of the pne

Exercises To Improve Your Poture, Why Is Posture o mportant?

Having a good posture is more important than looking good. It helps you develop trength, flexblety, and balance n your body. All of them can lead to less mucle pain and more energy throughout the day.

Proper posture also reduces stress on your muscles and ligaments, which can lower your risk of injury.

Improving your posture also helps you become more aware of your muscles, making it easier to correct your posture. As you work on your posture and become more aware of your body, you may notice some imbalances or areas of tension that you were previously unaware of.

Read and to learn how 12 exercise that will assist you in understanding lttle taller.

1. A child's one

The retching pose stretches and lengthens your pne, glute, and hamstrings. The child's pose aids in the release of tension in the lower back and neck.

To accomplish this, first:

- Sit on your shinbones with your knees together, your big toes touching, and your heels splayed out to the side
- Fold forward at your hips and walk your hands out in front of you.
- Sink your hips back down toward your feet. If your thighs won't go all the way down, place a pillow or folded blanket under them for support.
- Gently place your forehead on the floor or turn your head to one side.
- Keep your arms extended or rest them along your body.
- Breathe deeply into the back of your rib cage and waist.
- Relax in this pose for up to 5 minutes while continuing to breathe deeply.

2.Forward Fold

This standing stretch releases tension in your spine, hamstrings, and glutes. It also stretches your hips and legs. While doing this stretch, you should feel the entire backside of your body opening up and lengthening. To do this:

- Stand with your big toes touching and your heels slightly apart.
- Bring your hands to your hips and fold forward at your hips

- Release your hands toward the floor or place them on a block. Don't worry if your hands don't touch the ground just go as far as you can.
- Bend your knees slightly, soften your hips joints, and allow your spine to lengthen.
- Tuck your chin into your chest and allow your head to fall heavily to the floor
- Remain in this pose for up to 1 minute.

3.Cat-Cow

Practicing cat-cow stretches and massages your spine. It also helps to relieve tension in your torso, shoulders, and neck while promoting blood circulation. To do this:

- Come onto your hands and knees with your weight balanced evenly between all four points
- Inhale to look up, dropping your abdomen down toward the ground as you extend your spine
- Exhale and arch your spine toward the ceiling and tuck your chin into your chest
- Continue this movement for at least 1 minute.

4. Standing Cat-Cow

Doing the cat-cow stretch while standing helps to loosen uptightness in your back, hips, and glutes.

To do this :

- Stand with your feet about hip-width apart with a slight bend in your knees.
- Extend your hands in front of you or place them on your thighs.
- Lengthen your neck, bring your chin toward your chest, and round your spine

- Then look up, lift your chest, and move your spine in the opposite direction.
- Hold each position for 5 breaths at a time.
- Continue this movement for a few minutes.

5. Chest Opener

This exercise allows you to open and stretch your chest. This is especially useful if you spend most of your day sitting, which tends to make your chest move inward. Strengthening your chest also helps you stand up straighter.

To do this:

- Stand with your feet about hip-width apart.
- Bring your arms behind you and interlace your fingers with your palms pressing together. Grasp a towel if your hands don't reach each other.
- Keep your head, neck, and spine in one line as you gaze straight ahead.
- Inhale as you lift your chest toward the ceiling and bring your hands toward the floor.
- Breathe deeply as you hold this pose for 5 breaths.
- Release and relax for a few breaths.
- Repeat at least 10 times.

6. High Plank

The high plank pose helps to relieve pain and stiffness throughout your body while strengthening your shoulders, glutes, and hamstrings. It also helps you develop balance and strength in your core and back, both important for good posture.

To do this:

- Come onto all fours and straighten your legs, lift your heels, and raise your hips.

55

- Straighten your back and engage your abdominal, arm, and leg muscles
- Lengthen the back of your neck, soften your throat, and look down at the floor
- Make sure to keep your chest open and your shoulders back.
- Hold this position for up to 1 minute at a time.

7. Side Plank

You can use a side plank to maintain the neutral alignment of your pne and leg. The energizing pose works the muscles in your de and glutes. Strengthening and aligning these muscles helps to support your back and improve posture.

To accomplish this:

- Bring your left hand lightly nto the center from a high plank poton.
- Shft your weght onto your left hand, tack your ankles, and left your hp.
- Place your right hand on your hp or extend your hand toward the celng.
- You can drop your left knee to the flood for extra upport.
- Engage your abdominals, de body, and glutes a you mantan the poe.
- Line your body from the crown of your head to your heels.
- Look traght ahead of you or up toward your hand.
- Hold the poe for up to 30 seconds.
- Rep on the opposite side.
- Downward-Facing Dog

8.Downward-Facing Dog

This is a forward bend that can be used as a resting spot to balance your body. The downward-facing dog can help releve back pan while also trengthening and algning your back mucle. Practising it regularly helps to improve posture.

To do this:

- Lyng wth your tomach on the flood, pre nto your hand and tuck your toe under your feet, and left your heel.
- Lift your knees and hp to bring your ting bone up toward the celng.
- Blend your knees and lengthen your spine.
- Keep your ears n line wth your upper arm or tuck your chn nto your chet.
- Press firmly into your hand and keep your heel lightly lifted.
- Stay in this position for up to one minute.

9. Pgeon Pose

This is a hip opener that also stretches your spine, hamstrings, and glute. The pgeon poe can alo help to stretch your catc nerve and quadriceps. Opening and stretching these places on your body makes it easier to correct imbalances in your posture.

To accomplish this:

- Come down on all four wth your knee below your houlder and your hand a lttle bt in front of your houlder.
- Bend your right knee and place it behind your right wrist, with your right foot angled out to the left.
- Ret your right shin on the floor.
- Slet your left leg back, straighten your knee, and ret your through on the floor.

- Make sure your left leg extends straight back (not to the side).
- Slowly lower your torso to ret on your ner right this with your arm extended in front of you.
- Hold this poton for up to one minute.

Slowly releae the potion by walking your hand back toward your hips and lifting your toro.

Rep on the left side.

10. Thoracic Spine Rotation

The exercise relieves tightness and pain in your back while increasing stability and mobility.

To do this:

- Come on all four and NK your hp back to your heels and rest on your shins.
- Place your left hand behind your head, elbow extended to the side.
- Keep your right hand under your shoulder or bring it to the centre and rest on your forearm.
- xhale a you rotate your left elbow toward the ceiling and stretch the front of your toro.
- Take a long nhale and exhale in the position.
- Releae back down to the organc potion.
- Rep the movement 5 to 10 times.
- Rep on the opposite side.

11. Glute S ueeze

This exercise helps to strengthen and activate your glutes while relieving lower back pain. It also improves the functionality and alignment of your hp and pelv, resulting in better performance.

To do this:

- Le on your back wth your knees bent and your feet about hip-distance apart.
- Keep your feet about a foot away from your hip.
- Ret your arms along your body wth your palm facing down.
- xhale a you branch your feet closer to your hp.
- Hold the poton for 10 econdS and then move them away from your hp.

Continue the movement for 1 minute.

Do this exercise a few times per day.

12. Iometrc rows

Exercie helps relieve pain and tffne from sitting in one place for too long. The iometrc pull works your houlder, arm, and back mucle, giving you the strength to maintain good posture.

To do thing:

- Sit n a char wth a oftback.
- Bend your arm so that your fingers are facing forward and your palms are facing each other.
- Exhale a you draw your elbow back nto the char behIND you and ueeze your houlder blade together.
- Breathe deeply as you hold the position for 10 seconds.
- Slowly release to the tartng poton on an nhale.
- Rep this movement for 1 minute.
- Do this exercise every tyme throughout the day.

CHAPTER 5:

HOW BODY LANGUAGE REVEALS EMOTION

What Your Body Is Doing Your Language Reveal

Whether you're presenting on tage or networkng at a trade conference, debating a project with a coworker, or detecting someone's lie, body language is often the key to create or uncover, the

Body language became a significant part of your life long before you aid your first word. I concluded that body language accounts for 55 per cent of all communication. People intuitively and intantaneouly develop a perception in the first moment they see you, and their body language builds, confirms, or dimples those impressions. With that in mind, here a few feelings you may have experienced while watching other people around the office, or

60

everyone else may have felt while Use thie information to improve your understanding of the world around you and increase the effectiveness of your credibility, communication.

You're either lying or extremely nervous

A lie, nervoune, or fear in Wetern culture can be ymptomatic of a lie, nervoune, or fear. Sweating, shaking, licking lips, and moving the hand to the face to cover the mouth or eye are other ignal. Unfortunately, lying can sometimes be confused with a bad case of butterflie, but it can also make perfect sense. When someone lies, they uually don't have confidence in their meage, and their body reveals that. When you're nervous, you simply lack elf-aurance and it how.

Headed right to the top

Charisma. Energy. you contact. Open the body language. These are the signs of success and of someone who understands how to communicate.

well well with their body They approach you with an assertive handshake, can sit calmly while still exerting energy, align themselves with the room when speaking, and have complete control over their movement and gestures.

Yawn

Boredom can be detected from a mile away. When people go into standby mode, they tend to focus on the important thing, such as drawing a q uiggle, staring off into space, or reading the word on their pen. Boredom is difficult to conceal because it represents a conflict between one's unconscious desires and physical presence. Look for the placid facial expreion or the peron who han't made eye contact for the last 20 minute, and then chek for a pulse or signs of life.

Why don't you just Roll ver?

ubmiive peron's body language displays helplene The physical sign of an overly-forgiving person manifests when a person is anxious and wishes to avoid any form of criticism or conflict. They have a heepih look on their face, remain relatively till to avoid drawing attention to themselves, and may keep their face

You've got my attention.

Interet What this doesn't entail is checking your smartphone neakily beneath the table or repeatly glancing at your watch. We frequently liten or watch, but we don't take it in, process it, and tore the information. When you get omeon's attention, they are proactive recipients with proactive body language.

How Body Language Reveals The Real You

Body language is an often-overlooked aspect of communication that is critical to supporting your spoken words and messages. although most of the time it occurs automatically, you can learn to learn to learn to learn to learn to learn to learn to learn to learn to manage your poture, facial expreion, and geture actively, and it can have an incredibly powerful effect on your ability to communicate. Mater your body language and you will certainly develop a deeper undertanding of the people around you and dratically improve the impact of your in-peron

What Exactly Is Body Language?

Simply put, body language is the unspoken element of communication that we use to express our true feelings and emotions. For instance, our geture, facial expreion, and poture. We can use these signs to our advantage if we can "read" them. For example, it can help u to undertand the complete meage of what omeone I trying to ay to us and enhance our awarene of people'

We can also use it to adjust our body language so that we appear more positive, engaging, and approachable.

What body language do I have?

Body language entails more than jut the louch-factor or where you place your hands. It includes facial expression, proximity to others, body posture, habits, eye gestures, how we touch ourselves and others, how we interact with what we touch (i.e., fiddling), and even breathing.

Difficult Convergence and Defense

Difficult or tense conversations are an uncomfortable fact of work life. Perhaps you've had to deal with a difficult customer or needed to speak with someone about his or her poor performance. Or perhaps you've negotiated a major contract. Ideally, these ituation would be resolution calmly. However, they are frequently accompanied by feelings of nervoune, stress, defenivene, or even anger. And, despite our best efforts to conceal them, these emotions frequently surface in our body language. For example, if one exhibits one or more of the following behaviors, he will likely be diengaged, diintereted, or unhappy:

- Arm flowed in front of the body
- Minimal facial expression or tene facial expression
- The body turned away from you.
- yes downcat, maintaining le contact

Avoiding Unengaged Audiences

When you need to deliver a presentation or collaborate in a group, you want the people around you to be 100 percent engaged. Here are some "telltale" signs that may bore or confuse people about what you're saying:

- With head downcast, I sat slumped.

63

- Gazing at other things or into space.
- Fidgeting, picking at clothes, or fiddling with pen and phone.
- Doodling or writing

How to project a positive body Language

When you use positive body language, you can add trength to the verbal messages or ideas you want to convey and avoid sending mixed or conflicting signals. In this section, we will describe some basic postures that you can use to project self-confidence and openness. Making a Confidential First Impression These tips can help you adjust your body language to make a great first impreion:

1. **Possess n pen Posture:** Be relaxed, but don't louch! Sit or stand upright and place your hands by your side. Avoid standing with your hand on your hip; this will make you appear larger, which can communicate disagreement or a desire to dominate.
2. **Use Firm Handhake:** However, don't get carried away! You don't want it to be awkward or, worse, painful for the other person. If it does, you will most likely be labelled as rude or aggressive.
3. **Good Maintain Contact:** ye Contact: ye Contact: ye Contact Try to hold the other person's gaze for a few seconds at a time. This will demonstrate to her that you are sincere and engaged. But don't turn it into a taring match!
4. **Avoid Touching our Face:** There is a widely held belief that people who touch their faces while answering questions are dishonest. While this isn't always true, it's best to avoid fiddling with your hair or touching your mouth or nose, especially if you want to come across as trustworthy.

Public Speaking:

Positive body language can also help you engage people, make preentation nerve, and project confidence when you peak in public. Here are a few pointers to get you started:

1. **Possess a Positive Posture**: Sit or tand upright, with your houlder back and your arm at your sides or in front of you. Don't try to put your hand in your pocket or to louch, as this will make you appear uninterested.
2. **keep ur head up**: Your head hould be level and upright. Leaning forward or backward can make you look aggreive or arrogant.
3. **Perfect our Poture and Practice**: You'd practise your presentation beforehand, so why not practice your body language as well? Stand in a relaxed manner, well-distributed weight. Keep one foot slightly in front of the other – this will help you maintain your posture.
4. **Geture Ue Open Hand**: Spread your hand apart, in front of you, with your palm facing le toward your audience. This indicates a willingness to communicate and share ideas. Keep your upper limbs close to your body. Take care to avoid overexposure, or people may pay more attention to your hand than to what you're saying.

Key Points

The nonverbal ignal that you ue to communicate your feelings and intentions is referred to as body language. It includes your poture, facial expreion, and your hand geture. The ability to understand and interpret body language can help you pick up a job.

on an unspoken iue, problem, or negative feeling that other people may have You can also use it in a positive way to add strength to your verbal messages.

Body Language Negative nclude:

- arm flowed
- facial expression tene
- The body turned away from you.
- Poor eye contact.

Positive body Language Incluedes:

- OPEN body position (not flowed arm).
- Proper posture.
- Relaxed and open to facial exploration.
- The ide relaxed the rm hanging.
- eye contact on regular ba.

Being Deliberate in Your Display of Body Language

While you cannot control your facial microexpressions, you can control your body language. Using body language in communication allows us to convey all of our subtleties and nuances about ourselves in an efficient yet impactful manner. How you move your body speaks louder than words ever could. Whether you are aware of it or not, it has the potential to harm your reputation and personal brand.

We need to be cautious because our body language can end mixed ignal if we don't pay attention. When we are not mindful of how we present ourselves, we can send a message that is not aligned with our intent. This is then picked up by another without us even realizing it, and it all happens in an instant. Consider a new acquaintance who is nervous and a little socially awkward. On his first day, he walks through the office with his arms crossed, trying to hide I uncomfortablene. He's a nice guy, but he's nervous about the new situation. While this is understandable, his body language is telling others that he is closed off and possibly untruthful.

Best Ways to Communicate Via Body Language

Whether you feel it or not, try to have your body language convey a sense of confidence, ease, relatability, and warmth.

1. Posture

Be aware of how you sit and stand. Maintain a tall pine with your houlder back and your head slightly elevated. The inverse of this posture is what you probably look like when you're checking your phone. With your eyes down, your head bowed, and your shoulders hunched, you may appear small and hunched. While everyone is doing it, it's not a good look. Try to overcome the tendency to appear in this manner.

2. Hands Utilization

A firm and confident handshake is a no-brainer. But it's probably more important to be mindful of what you do with your hands once the handshake is over. Display confidence or ease by simply keeping your hand at your side or behind your back. Croing them in front of you demonstrate being cloed off or defensive. Refrain from touching your face, as this can make you appear ecure or uncomfortable.

3. Eye Contact

When speaking with others, look them in the eyes. It demonstrates aurance and interest. However, read your converation partner(). Some people are unaffected by prolonged eye contact. Break away frequently to look at a ditant object before resuming eye contact. Rep this cycle. You may break away more or

67

les fre q uently depending on the read of your conversation partner.

4. Facial xpressions

This I the mot popular way of expreing emotion through the body. It includes eye, eyebrow, lip, noe, and cheek movement. We look to face for information and ocial connection from birth, and they can go a long way in helping u bond by diplaying empathy. Smiling with a reassuring nod while someone is telling a good story, or grimacing and shaking your head when hearing something difficult.

To build rapport with others faster, ubtly copy their body language using a techni q ue called mirroring. Because conversation partners see their geture and mannerim in your body language, they naturally put them at ease. This needs to be done ubtly for it to work! Otherwise, they'll think you're weird.

Final Thoughts

Often, the meage conveyed through our body language peak volume and in way, our words cannot express. It can betray our honet emotions whether we know it or not, and it's the magic that can accelerate forming our deeper relationships. For something that carries uch meaning, our body language diplayed for the world to interpret deerve equally our attention while we convey with accuracy our

Take action!

Give some thought to how you communicate nonverbally. There is a great resource that breaks down all nonverbal communication. This exercise may be was helpful to do with one who knows you well becaue it's hard to recognize how we're

68

perceived by other. Determine your body language strength and area of opportunity after the exercise.

Decoding The Throat

If someone is smiling, that's a good sign, right? Not necessarily. Different miles mean different things. The same is true for someone's lip position.

Smiles

- With a true, genuine smile, the corners of the mouth turn up, and the eyes narrow and wrinkle at the corners.
- Inincere smiles don't generally nvolve the eyes. They can happen in response to decomfort. A mirk or a partial mile that follows a microexpreion of dipleaure or contempt can suggest uncertainty, didain, or dislike.
- A mile accompanied by lating eye contact, a long glance, or a head tilt can suggest attraction.

Lip

- compressed or narrowed lip can suggest uneae.
- Fear or sadness can be indicated by quivering lips.
- Pured lips may indicate agreement or diagreement.
- Open, lightly parted lips tend to mean that someone feels relaxed or generally at ease.

The Eyes Can Say A lot

A lot of ye can convey a lot of information about someone's mood and level of interest.

Blinking

People tend to blink quickly when they are under some kind of tre. You may have heard that rapid blinking often indicates

69

dishonesty, but this is not always the case. Some people's blinking may speed up when they're:

- working through a difficult problem
- Uncomfortable feeling
- fraid or worried about something

Dilation of the Pupil

When you feel positively toward something or someone, your pupil will typically dilate. These feelings may involve romantic attraction, but this is not always the case. Dilation occurs in response to the arousal of your nervous system, so you may notice dilated pupils when someone is angry or afraid. When you don't like something, your student wilt contract or get maller.

Gaze definition

Your eye tend to follow what you're intereted in, so tracking the movement of someone's gaze can give you information about their mood. If you're talking to someone whose eyes keep wandering toward the buffet table, they may be more interested in eatng than talking. Someone standing near the exit may wish to leave. People tend to move their eyes down or to one ide when:

- Working troug through a problem
- Retrieving information or reminiscences
- Considering a Difficult Thing

Eye Blocking

It includes things such as:

- Covering your eyes with your hand
- loing your eye briefly, uch a uch a in a long blink
- Rubbing your eye with q uniting

Blocking I generally unconciou, but tends to suggest how you feel. People frequently block their eyes when they are irritated, distressed, or confronted with something they do not particularly want to do. It can also suggest disagreement or reluctance. You know the houe need a good cleaning, but when your partner sugget taking a day for chore, your hand may go to your eyes before you

Watching The arm and Legs

Although people uually use their arms and legs to make purpoeful geture, movement that happen more intinctively can also reveal

Arms

- Vulnerable
- Anxious
- Uninterested in considering another perspective

Intriguingly, crossed arms can alo sugget confidence. If someone croes their arm while smiling, leaning back, or howing other signs of being at ease, they probably feel omewhat in control of the ituation, rather than vulnerable. The arm can also give omeone a ene of protection. Keep an eye out for behaviors such as:

- Holding somether against the chest
- Bringing an arm to ret on a chair or table
- Using an arm to create distance
- ung one arm to hold the other back

These gestures subconsciously imply that a person does not feel entirely comfortable with the situation and needs to prepare or protect themselves in some way.

Legs and Feet

The feet and leg can see nervoune and retlene through:

- feet tapping
- jiggling legs
- Shifting from foot to foot

Crossed Legs can also indicate an unwillingness. to hear what other have to say, expecially when arm are alo croed Feet can also reveal information. Take note of the direction a peron's feet face during a conversation. If their feet point away, they may feel like leave the convertion than keep it. If their feet point toward you, the peron I likely enjoying the converation and wanting it to continue.

Hands

Many people ue gestures for emphai when speaking. This can have a direct benefit in that we tend to answer someone's question faster if they make gestures while aking. The more enthusiastic the gesture, the more excited someone is likely to feel. It's also fairly common for people to gesture toward someone they feel particularly close to, often without realizing it. Here are some more specific things to keep an eye out for.

- Outstretched hands with palms up may be an unintentional reflection of openne.
- Clenched fit can sugget anger or frutration, especially in one trying to uppre these emotion. You may notice that their facial experience remains neutral, even relaxed.
- Intuitively touching the cheek may indicate that someone I considering something carefully or has a lot of interest in what you're aying.

Breathing Clue

When you're stressed, your breathing tends to pick up. This tre can be positive or negative, so one breaking q uickly may be:

- Excited
- Anxious
- nervou or worried

A Long Deep Breath Can Suggestion:

- Relief
- Anger
- Fatigue

Slower breath typically suggest a tate of calm or thoughtfulne Ordinary breathing patterns may not stand out much, but someone else's breathing can eem very controlled or precise. This internal control occurs frequently when attempting to suppress a strong emotion, such as anger.

Posture

Your posture or the way you hold yourself, isn't always easy to control, which can make it difficult to read. It can still provide some insight, especially when it differs from how a person normally carries themselves.

Here are some things to look for:

- Leaning back on a wall or other upport can suggel boredom or diinteret.
- Leaning into a converation or toward someon typically suggests intreret or excitement.
- Standing up straight, sometimes with hand-on-hip, can suggest excitement, eagerness, and confidence. Standing

73

traight with hand at the sides I a common reting poition that uggets a wildness to engage and listen.

- Resting the head in one hand can mean interest. When both hands upport the head, boredom or fatigue may be suggested.
- Tilting the head or body to one ide suggetng INTeret and CONcentration. It can also sugget attraction depending on other body language marker.

Distance

The degree of physical distance a person maintain when talking to you can often give you clue about their mood or feeling for you. Keep in mind that many people simply prefer to keep more ditance between themelve and others, especially people they don't know well. On the other hand, some people may feel accutomed to less peronal pace. They may stand or very cloe becaue that' jut how they interact. That being said, some specific behaviour can be telling:

- Someone who regularly stands next to you or lives very close to you is likely to enjoy your company. Someone who stands apart and take a teep forward if you take a teep forward likely want to maintain ome ditance (physical and emotional) from you.
- Sitting close enough to touch or leaning into a conversation, especially with a mile or brief touch, often suggests phyical attraction.
- Putting up a hand or arm when taking a teep back frequently indicates a desire for a physical barrier or more ditance.

Putting together all

Body language can be complex and difficult to understand. There is an entire field of study called kineic that is dedicated to understanding nonverbal communication. Slight changes in intance and facial expression tend to happen naturally during a converation or ocial interaction. However, one with a contently erect poture or fixed expression may put in a lot of effort to keep their true emotions from showing. If you're having trouble understanding body language, keep the following tips in mind:

1 **Speak To Them**: It never hurts to ak one how they feel. If you notice a restless foot or a clenched fit, try pulling them aside and asking if everything is okay.

2 **Consider Their Previous Body Language**: Body language varies from person to person. If someone's unique body language uddenly eem different, it's a clue that omething may be going on beneath the urface.

3 **I'm for Some levels of ye ontact**: You don't have to tare or maintain continuou eye contact, but it helps to meet someone's gaze and hold it for the better part of a When you're looking at the person, you're more likely to pick up on body language.

4 **Remember to lite**n: Listening is always a part of good communication. Don't get so caught up in trying to decipher someone's gesture or position that you forget to listen to their words.

In general speaking, you can't get a complete picture of what other think and feel baed on their body language alone. When you put body language in the context of their word, you may get a lot more information than you would when conidering either

Caveats of Body Language

Before we get into the specific methods for improving your body language, remember that no one geture is univeral. Ithough a crossed arm can indicate a communication blockage, it can also be a source of confusion.

needed for warmth or jut a comfortable way to hold your arm Rubbing your eyes could mean you're tired or have an itch, or it could simply mean you're tired or have an itch. Try not to read into body language (yours or others') too much or too literally.

Culture alo played a part in body language. Some cultures value personal space more than others, so proximity guideline would differ depending on who you're dealing with. Other cultures see eye contact as a threat and a lack of respect, rather than the sign of confidence that many people see. As western culture view it as.

Ways to Improve Your Body Language

Here are 16 ways to understand and improve your body language.

1   Be aware

The first step toward bettering one's body language is awareness. Begin paying attention to everything you do and when you do it. The other day, I noticed I play with my earring when talking to certain people or about certain topic; with that realization, I can better undertand why Half the battle is wareness.

2   Other study

76

Look at other people, especially people you admire. How do they keep themselves together? What can you learn from them?

3   Mirror the other person

If you are sitting or standing opposite someone, mirror their body positions, match their tone, and carry the same pace of the conversation. Don't do it in an obvious or unnatural manner. Subtle mirroring can create a synergy and connection, and after a while, you'll be doing it naturally you'll not know who I following who!

4   Be Aware of How You Cross Your rm & Leg

Many people find croing arms or legs comfortable, so saying you can't do it is pointless. If you want to cro your legs, that's fine; just be careful aware of the direction you cro them in, and make certain you cro towards your conversation partner. Be aware that crossing your leg in a "figure four" fashion with your ankle resting on your knee can be perceived as tubborn or arrogant.

5   Make your contact

Yees are windows into the soul, and what you do with them communicates a lot. Be sensitive to culture that eschew eye contact with elders or tranger; otherwie, don't be afraid to look omeone in the eye. You will not only make a lot of money, but you will also learn a lot.

6   Relax, Shoulders.

Holding your houlder by your ear I a sign of tenion, and tand to put your converation partner on edge as well.

7   Don't be a slacker.

Ithough sitting ram-rod traight may be a forced exaggeration, ensure you're not slouching. Your back and social life will benefit.

8   Confront Your Converation Partner

Not facing your converation partner, like croing arms and leg, I a sign of distraction or disinterest. By facing your partner, you will increase engagement.

9   In lean

Have you ever had a converation that you're all enthuiatic about? You'll probably notice that you're both lively and leaning towards each other.

10   Take Care of Your Fidgeting

I'm a ucker for playing with my draw, traw, earring, or bottle cap with what I affectionately refer to as "tactile fixation." However, it can be a sign of nervoune and, at the very least, a distraction for others. Also, avoid touching your face or running your hands through your hair.

11   Don't Tilt Your Head (Too Far)

Ithough a lilt tilt of your head can indicate interest, too much head tilt (women are the main culprit for this) indicates ubmiivene.

12   Do not nd Sentence With Upwing

Although intonation isn't a body language, it warrant mentioning becaue it's part of the ubconciou messages we communicate. nding your sentences like questions indicate a lack of confidence in what you're ayining, which does not instil others' confidence in you.

13   Go For Firm r Matching Handshake

Do not q ueeze the life out of your new ac q uaintance, but a nice firm handshake feel good. Except for wet fishes, I tend to match my acquaintance's handhake (like mirroring). I simply cannot do it.

14 Know Where Your Hands Are

Holding your arm behind your back with your hand clasped is a sign of confidence. (It also gives you something to do with your hands if you're a gambler!) This is excellent for public speaking.) Holding your hands in your pocket may be comfortable, but it can alo indicate boredom or over-confidence.

15 Sit In an Engaging position

Unless your tar-croed lovers game into one another' eyes, sitting directly opposite omebody indicate confrontion. It's even wore wlth a table or dek between you, which creates a barrier. Instead, try it at a 45-degree angle. This provides comfort, and space, and still allows you to mirror and engage.

16 Relax!

Take a deep breath and relax now that you're probably hyper-aware of everything you do and don't do. Changing your body language may feel unnatural at first, so don't push it too hard. Using a doe of awarene and applying thee techniques gently over time, you'll communicate everything you want to word and your body.

Body Language Technology to Improve Your PUBLIC SPEaking

The value of good body language cannot be overstated. It is extremely important not only to audience engagement but also to how your overall message is received. No matter how good your speech is, if you are motionless, emotionless, and dull, your audience will lose interest within minutes. To help you master your body language, I have compiled a quick and simple tip.

Posture

- Maintain good posture by standing straight with your shoulders back, relaxed, and your feet houlder-width apart.
- Do not Cross your arm, put your hand in your pocket, or louch.
- Face the audience as much as possible and keep your body open.

Breathing

- Relaxed and deep breathing ensures that your voice has power and can project.
- Use slow and measured breathing to place your peech, paue to emphaize key point.

Gestures

- To emphaize your word, use hand geture.
- Keep the audience's attention by varying your gesturing, including your head, arm, and hand.
- Use positive geture to way your audience.
- When using visual aids, point and look at the relevant data.
- The audience will automatically follow your hand and eye movements.

Eye ontact

- Moving from face to face and maintaining eye contact while speaking ensures that the audience is engaged.
- When anwering an audience member' q uetion, maintain eye contact, this convey sincerity and credibility.

Movement

- As you move around the presentation area, your peech will become more dynamic.

- Use movement to illustrate tranition from one subject to another.
- Stepping toward the audience create a positive feeling, ue this techni q ue when you want to encourage or persuade your audience.

Facial expreion

A simple smile will make your audience feel more at ease and comfortable.

Bring them all together

While we all want to believe that standing alone in front of a room is natural, it is not natural to stand alone in front of a group of people. It's an odd and unusual thing that causes tre, tension, and stomach problems. Being natural will not cut it. We need to be bigger, more expressive, and more powerful. It necessitates a great deal of effort and energy. It also necessitates skill and practice. With so much reliance on communication, and communication reliant on body language, it's worth getting it right. Work on your body language-geture, tance, and facial expression to make the most of every speaking opportunity.

You Must Avoid Body Language Mistakes

You are a master communicator as an event professional. Just look at all the email and phone calls you've made the precedent week. With all that writing and talking, you get the sense that you're good with words. But how language does your body language language language language

Your body language has a significant impact on how clients, vendors, and coworkers perceive you. If you don't watch yourelf, you could be bored, disinterested, lazy, or dishonest. The following

81

list may contain some items you've heard of before, but others are so obscure that you've probably never heard of them.

Weak Handshakes

This one usually goes without saying, but it's important enough to mention. Weak handshake makes you look weak. Begin a meeting with firm handshakes to show that you are confident and capable. Concerned that your hands will become weaty? Discreetly dry them against your pant leg while greeting the peron. They will be paying attention to your face and will not notice the gesture, and you will have the confidence to shake hands firmly.

Leading Back

It turned out that your high school teacher had a reason you leaned back in your chair after lunch, and it wan't jut becaue you lost your balance once a week. This body language indicates that you are disinterested and daydreamy. This body language I offenive at all times, but especially when you are supported to be listening to omeone speak as it can be interpreted

Slouching

Slouching and allowing your body to fold in on itelf makes you appear weak and unenergetic. This is a terrible impression to make, especially in a high-energy profesion like event planning. Instead, tand or houlder back your back traight and houlder back. This traight poture will help you appear capable, confident, and energized.

Crossing Your arms (Or Legs)

Crossing your arms in any way makes you appear closed off or unwilling to negotiate. It can even be interpreted a combative and rude Instead of crossing your arms, let them relax gently at your sides or on the dek/table next to you. This demonstrates that you are relaxed and open to other people's suggestions. Croing your leg can be interpreted imally, so be aware of your leg are vible not to it with croed legs.

The Feet Point Way

Did you know that your feet point in the direction you want to go? When a person is listening intently to another person, his or her feet will point toward them. If he or he is ready to go to lunch, he or he will shift to a point towards the door. Make ure you pay attention to the meage your feet are ending when they are visible.

Changing way

Your body, like your feet, will point to where it is focused. If you want to make a strong impression, move your body lightly to angle toward whoever I speaking dure a meeting. It doesn't have to be a big change, especially if the meeting involves a lot of people taking turns speaking. Nonetheless, the ubtle shift is worthwhile. People are unlikely to notice consciously, but they will think you're a great listener.

Hide Your Hands

Standing with your hand behind your back in your pockets is extremely common, but it results in a bad meage. Subconsciously, the people you are with may interpret that you have something to hide. This is also the case when sitting at a desk or table with your hand on your lap. Instead, keep your hand where they are visible and learn to be comfortable with them at your side or in front of you.

Fidgeting

Fidgeting, whether you are playing with your hair, shuffling papers, or tapping your foot, I a great way to come acro an underprepared, anxious, If you have a difficult time sitting still in a meeting, become a great note-taker. Just be careful not to get lot doodling as a symbole of disinterest! Feel free to geture when you talk to keep your hand buy during converation; just don't overdo it.

Geture Exaggerated

Are you wondering why you shouldn't overdo the gestures? While small gestures make you appear to be a good leader who is passionate about what you do, exaggerated gestures can make you appear arrogant. When gesturing, be careful of the personal space of thoe around you.

Never get so carried away with your hands that you accidentally bump someone. If you're not sure whether your gestures are offensive, ask a friend to videotape you while you're having a conversation. Then, play it back and see what you think. You can keep geturing; just have the boiterou motion for your next scene onstage.

Touching Your Face

This I probably the mot urprie body language mistake on the lit! You probably believe that putting your hand on your chin makes you look intelligent or as if you are thinking carefully. It turns out that touching your face makes you look dihonet, especially if your hand is touching your mouth or noe.

Self-Soothing

There are many ways people elf-oothe subconsciously. Some people wrap their ankles or leg around table legs. Some people clasp their hands together. Others place their hand on their thigh or fidget with their clothing's fabric. While these activities and poture may make you feel more at eae in an uncomfortable situation, they don't make you look trong. Self-oothing makes you appear weak and anxious. If you are uncomfortable in a situation, try to figure out what is causing your discomfort and address it so that you can be more confident without self-soothing.

WATCHING THE TIME (OR YOUR PHONE)

Better, you know. Do not do it. Maintain the urge to check the clock or your phone during an individual or group meeting. If you need to check your phone because you are expecting an important call or message, let the person or group know ahead of time and apologize. If you need to leave at a specific time, notify them and set an alarm to vibrate on your phone 5 or 10 minutes before you need to leave. People wonder if they know what's going on, but checking the clock or your phone during a meeting implies that you have more important things to do.

The absence of mirroring

People who are liitening intently to someone unconciouly mirror their body language. If the peron you are litening to have their hand folded, you wilt likely have their hand folded. If he tilts his head to the left, you will most likely tilt your head to the right to mirror his behaviour. This is something that happens without conscious thought, and the reverse is also true. If you aren't litening, you aren't mirroring body language. Learn to use this to your advantage by intentionally mirroring the body language of the person speaking to you.

Eye Contact avoiding

Avoiding eye contact makes you appear untrustworthy. Look someone in the eye when you're listening to them. When you're talking to someone, look them in the eyes. When addressing a crowd, move your gaze throughout the audience so that everyone feels included. Taking the time to provide proper eye contact makes you appear confident and trustworthy.

Too many eye contact

There is always a flip ide, and this is no exception. voiding eye contact is a big no-no, but o is too many eye contact. Looking someone in the eyes too much makes you appear adverarial and intense. I'm only available for 10 seconds at a time. Be sure to break eye contact every few seconds, but come back to see how you're still engaged. When breaking eye contact, look to the ide rather than to the ide rather than to the ide rather than down a look down how weakness while look ideway how confidence

CHAPTER 6:

HOW TO READ AND IDENTIFY EMOTIONS

What Exactly Is Motion?

The term "emotion" is quite broad and even ambiguous - it encompasses a wide range of aspects of experience:

Feelings: Which I mean body states' perception or experience. For example, fear causes your heart to pound.

Pattern for THOUGHT & THINKING: I mean particularly inner dialogue by thought. In anger, for example, you have thought about revenge. They are also thinking tyle - in deprivation, thinking is slow and repetitive.

Urge & mpule T oct: When you're angry, you're compelled to yell or even hit out.

Attention: You tend to focu in particular ways and on particular things - e.g., in anxiety, you focu rather narrowly on what

The ability to read emotion from a person's face is a very important skill. One could even call it a superpower. People all over the world use this kill when they communicate with one another. But, do people from diferent cultural background recognize and INTerpret facial expreion the ament? According to cientit, the answer is both yes and no. Yes, because the brain ytem pecializing in undertanding face is imilar acro culture, we all can recognize baic emotions, uch a happine or sadness when looking No, because culture influences how we behave and think, which means it also influences the rules we learn as children that tell us when and how to express our emotions. In this article, we discuss how we can read emotion from face and how we may be reading emotion differently depending on where we are. motional literacy it the ability to understand your writen feelings, listen to others and empathize with their feelings, and express emotion productively

What are you feeling right now as you begin to read this? Are you interested? I'm hoping you'll learn something about yourself. Bored because this is something you have to do for school and you're not really into it, or happy because it's a school project you enjoy? Maybe you're distracted by something else, like being excited about your weekend plans or sad because you just went through a breakup. Such emotions are a part of human nature. They inform you about what we are experiencing and help you understand how to react.

We remember our emotions from when we were babies. Infant and young children express their emotions through facial expressions or actions such as laughing, cuddling, or crying. They know what they feel and how they feel, but they can't name the emotion or explain why they feel that way. As we grew older, we became better at understanding emotions. Instead of simply reacting to what a small child does, we can identify what we are feeling and put it into words. With time and practice, we become better at knowing what we are feeling and why. This ability is known as emotional awareness.

Motivational awareness helps us know what we need and want (or don't want!). It helped us better relationhip That's because being aware of our emotions can help us talk about them more clearly, avoid or resolve conflicts better, and move past difficult feelings more easily. Some people are naturally more in touch with their emotions than others. The good news is that everyone can be more aware of their emotions. It just takes practice. But it's well worth the effort: motional awarene I the first term toward building emotional intelligence, a skill that can help people succeed in life.

Here are a few fundamentals about motivation:

1. Emotions Come and Go: Most of us experience a wide range of emotions throughout the day. Some lated only a few seconds. Others may linger to become a mood.

2. motivion an Be Mild, Intense, r nywhere n Between: The intensity of an emotion can vary depending on the situation and the person.

3. There are no good or bad emotions, but there are good and bad ways of experiencing (recting n) emotions: Learning how to expre emotion in a acceptable way I a eparate kill managing emotion that are built on a foundation of being able

It'll Be Good

1. Some emotions are positive, such as being happy, loving, confiding, inspired, cheerful, interested, grateful, or included. Other emotions can be more negative, such as being angry, resentful, afraid, ashamed, sad, or worried. Both positive and negative emotions are normal.

2. All emotions tell you something about yourself and your situation. But it can be difficult to accept what we feel at times. We may judge ourselves for feeling a certain way, such as if we feel jealou, for example. Instead of thinking that we shouldn't feel that way, it's better to recognize how we feel.

3. Avoiding negative feelings or pretending we don't feel the way we do can backfire. It's more difficult to move past difficult feelings and allow them to fade if we don't confront them and try to understand why we feel that way. You don't have to dwell on your emotions or constantly talk about how you feel. motional awarene simply means recognizing, respecting, and accepting your feelings as they occur.

Creating motional awarenes

Emotional awareness helps us understand and accept ourselves. So, how can you become more aware of your emotions? Begin with these three easy technology technology technology technolog

1. Develop the habit of tuning in to how you feel in various situations throughout the day: You might notice that you feel excited after making a plan to go omewhere with a friend. Or that you are nervou before an exam. When you relax, you may be relaxed.

Listening to music, being inspired by an art exhibit, or feeling relieved when a friend disappoints you. Simply notice whatever emotion you are experiencing and name it in your mind. It only takes a second to do this, but it's an excellent practice. Notice that each emotion passes and make room for the next experience.

2. Rate form an emotion, form an emotion, form an emotion, form Rate how strongly you feel the emotion on a scale of 1–10, with 1 being the mildest feeling and 10 being the most intense.

3. SHare your FEELINGS With the People loet To You: This is the best way to practice putting emotions into words, a skill that will help you feel closer to a friend, a boyfriend or a girlfriend, a parent, or anyone else. Make it a daily practice to share your feelings with a friend or family member. You could share something very personal or something that is simply an everyday emotion.

How to Identify Your Emotions and Why It's Important

You've probably heard that emotional intelligence is a key predictor of success in most, if not all, walks of life. motional intelligence is based on elf-awarene - the ability to feel emotion, to name them (emotional literacy), and to be overwhelme (Actually, being able to name emotion help you not be overwhelmed.) But how do you go about improving your emotional awarene and emotional literacy if you feel lacking? This article suggests one method.

How Does Culture Influence How We Express Our Emotions?

Human beings around the world have similar brain tructure and use similar facial mucles to express basic emotions such as happiness, sadness, fear, urprie, Does this imply that we all express and read each other's emotions in the same way?

According to cientit who tudy emotion, the answer is both yes and no. While many experienced have hown that people around the

Other research has shown that there are differences in the way people read facial expressions depnd on the way people read facial expressions. This make ene when we consider that people from diferent culture do not all behave and think the ame way.

People from various cultures analyze motion xpressions. Differently

Diplay rule not only tells us how and when to express emotions, but also influences how we ee and undertand emotions of others. For example, people are used to seeing faces that how a lot of trong emotions. In others, people are ued to face with less expreion, where diplay rule ay that emotions should not always be trongly expreed. When you see emotional expreion of similar trength often enough in your own culture, it influences the way you read emotion from facial expreion.

Superpower Training and Testing

Reading face is a superpower that gets bexter the more you learn about it and the more you practice it. There are also various games you can play with your friends to see who among you is better at reading emotions. For example, you could take a picture or card with face expreing different emotion (happy, angry, ad, surprised, afraid, diguted). Then someone can pull a card and try to enact the emotion from the card ung jut their faces. Others should guess which emotion the person with the card is attempting to convey. As a bonus, you will have the opportunity to hone your acting skills!

Developing Self-regulation and Emotional Intelligence

The app isn't just about increasing your emotional self-awareness; it's also about developing emotional regulation skills and, ultimately, greater emotional intelligence. So there are additional steps beyond identifying your emotion that I won't go into here. If you use it, lot over several day it can track your emotional tate and how you reports

Motion Reading

Humans communicate emotion through language, ound (or tone), facial expressions, and body language. Language and culture can have an impact on how people express their emotions. Regardless of differences, all humans experience certain key emotions. Your ability to read and respond to emotions in others is referred to as emotional intelligence. You can improve awareness of emotion in yourself and others by developing your emotional intelligence.

ANALIZE MOTION IN OTHER

1. Recognize Positive and Negative Human Motivation: There are Happiness, urprie, anger, fear, sadness, and digit are the six universal human emotions. These categorie fall into two categorie: Positive (happine, surprise) and negative (anger, fear, sadness, digit) emotions To distinguish them from others, you must first understand what kinds of actions and behaviours they are associated with. These are some examples:

1. Positive emotions reduce stress, improve mood, and increase memory and awareness. For instance, happine, urprie, sympathy, kindness, love, courage, confidence, inspiration, relief, etc.

2. Negative emotion increase tre, allow us to recognize threat, and deal with difficult situations. Examples include adne, fear, anger, contempt, digit, and so on.

3. The amygdala complex and the prefrontal cortex are the two more important region of the brain for expreing and undertanding emotion. Damage to either of these areas can impair someone's ability to read emotions.

2. Concentrate On The Ye nd MOUTH: People express their emotions through their eyes and/or mouths in general. Culture influences the region of the face in which a person displays emotion. People in Japan, for example, focus on their eyes, whereas people in the United States focus on their ears. United Interpret emotion I stated in the mouth. When reading emotion, look at their entire face rather than just the eye.

1. Stand far enough away to see their face, but have a normal conversation. between 1 1/2 to 4 feet I a good ditance to keep between you and the other peron.

3. Listen to the Tone of Voice: Following facial expreion, tone of voice is the econd most important way people expre emotion. People use their voices to express and control their emotions. However, some emotions are not conveyed via voice. People can easily identify relaxed, treed, boredom, contentment, and confidence from the tone of voice. Fear, friendliness, happine, and adne are just a few of the emotions that can be expressed weakly through tone of voice.

1. A similar tone of voice can express different emotions. A tene/harh voice, for example, is associated with anger and hotility, as well as a confidence and interet.

2. A whispery or soft tone of voice can be associated with a variety of emotions. These include relaxation, content, intimacy, friendship, adne, and boredom.

3. oft, breathy voice (where the person takes loud breathe while talking) is associated with fear, shyness, and nervoune.

4. Observe and NOTE General Behavior & Demeanor: Do they exude a friendly atmosphere when you look at them or are they more reserved? motion can be experienced unconciouly without you being aware of it. Using your best judgment and following your gut instincts can sometimes be the best way to read emotions.

1. Recognize emotion in others by noting your reaction. We frequently mirror the emotions of others in our facial expressions, tone of voice, and behaviour.

2. motion are valuable. We were affected by other people's emotions. Our mood and behavior vary dependent on how Someone else is feeling. This is why, if someone smiles at you, you are likely to smile back!

5. e The ther Peron' Physical Well-Being: Motivation can have an impact on health in both positive and negative ways. If a friend or family member is ick or tired all the time, they may be stressed-out or depreed.

1. Headache or migraine, low energy, tomach problems, back pain, changes in eating habits, alcohol or drug ue

2. Mental and emotional ymptomS of mental illne and depression include: confuion, udden and extreme mood change, iolation from friend, inability to cope with eve

6. Develop and improve our emotional intelligence: Teach yourself to recognize emotions in others by becoming more aware of your own. The four branches of emotional intelligence are as follows:

1. Be able to perceive emotion in yourself and others.

2. Make use of emotions to promote thinking.

3. Recognize the significance of emotion.

4. Manage emotion. Among the strategies for improving emotional intelligence are:

1. Download your phone and teep away from your computer. Improve your social skills and ability to read nonverbal cues by engaging in face-to-face communication daily.

2. Don't back away from uncomfortably or negatively charged feelings in yourself or others. These are important and necessary. If you're feeling sad or angry, take a step back and consider why you're feeling that way. Then, try to counteract the negative emotion with three positive ones.

3. Pay attention to your body: A knot in your tomach may be tre, or a fluttering heart may be attraction or excition.

4. Keep a journal or record of your thoughts and feelings. Stop a few times a week and write down what you're doing and how you're feeling. Other information, such as how much leep you had the night before, or what you had for breakfast, can be included.

5. Ask a close friend or family member – someone you know and trust – to read your emotions. Other people sometimes know us better than we know ourselves. Their answers can be both surprising and insightful.

FACIAL XPREION INTERPRETING

1. MAKE a note of their facial xpreion: How we feel inside is expressed in our eyes and on our faces. Learning to recognize the relationship between facial expression and specific types of emotion goes a long way toward being able to read emotion.

Don't be duped! People can manipulate their facial expreion to appear happy when they are angry or ad actor do the all the time. Look for other cues as to how they feel. Note their body language or voice tone. Make eye contact open, penetrating "cold" eye sugget a different emotional tate than a "warm" mile.

2. Recognize Genuine milé: genuine mile ue more muscles than one faked or forced. The mouth and cheek mouth and cheek mouth and cheek mouth and cheek mouth and cheek mouth and cheek If the skin around their eyes tightens and their "crow' feet" form (cluter of wrinkles around the outer corner of eye), it is a good indicator of a genuine smile.

3. Differentiah adne From Happine: This may seem obvious, but people try to control or cover up their true emotions by smiling when they are sad. Genuine and pontaneou emotion are difficult to fake. [30] Sadness is associated with frowning (lowering the

97

corner of the mouth). It is also associated with raising the inner corner of the eyebrow (near the nose). Additional cues are loose, drooping eyelids that cover a portion of the eye.

4. Recognize nger and Digit: Anger and disgust are frequently associated with one another and produce similar facial experiences. When we are irritated, angry, or annoyed, we wrinkle our noses.

1. anger and reentment can be toward one or about something. When we are angry, we droop our eyebrows, purge our lips (tighten them and uck-in the margin), and bulge our eyes.

2. In contrast to anger, expressing dislike, disgust, or disdain for someone or something associated with a raied upper lip and a loose lower lip. We also pull our eyebrow down, but not as much as when we are angry.

5. Recognize Fear and Surprising: While fear is a negative emotion and surprise is a positive emotion, both activate the sympathetic nervous system and trigger a "fight or flight" response. When something unexpected occurs, whether good or bad, it stimulates a part of the brain that is outside of our direct control. When thie happen, we pull up our eyebrow and eyelids to make our eyes wide open.

1. When we are afraid, we pull our eyebrow in (towards the noe), our pupil dilate (get better) to take in more light, and our mouth We tene up the mucle in our face, especially around our mouth and cheek.

2. When we arch our eyebrow and drop our jaw, we tend to arch our eyebrow and drop our jaw. Our mouth is open, and the mucus around it is relaxed and loose.

READING MOTION IN ANOTHER WAY

1. Be on the lookout for nonverbal ue: In addition to facial expression and tone of voice, humans express emotion in other ways. While nonverbal cues can be distracting, learning to pick them up can help you read emotions. Body movement, posture, and eye contact are important nonverbal cues that convey emotion. Make an effort to notice whether they appear animated and moving around or if they appear tiff and tense. lo, they tand up traight and make eye contact, hunch their shoulders, fidget with their hands, or cro their arm

1. Move around and stand up traight how they feel open and comfortable. However, excessive movement (e.g., energetic arm waving) combined with a loud voice could indicate that they are excited or agitated.

2. A hunched houlder, a quiet voice, and croed arms are a sign they feel uncomfortable or nervous. If they refuse to make eye contact with you, it could indicate that they are upset or feel guilty.

3. Remember that culture, social situation, and individual personality influence how we express emotion through body language. In this ene, facial expreion I regarded as more universal and reliable. For example, Italians tend to move their arms when they preach, but this could be considered impolite in Japan. Alternatively, making eye contact I a sign of repect in the United State and urope, but I considered rude or aggressive in ome ian and frican culture.

2. Observe Their Body Movement and Poture: The best way to read and transmit emotion is to focus on the entire body as well as the face. Poture and body movement, not only reflect emotion, both of emotion and emotion and emotion and emotion and emotion and emotion There are degrees of positive and negative emotion. For example, positive emotions range from intrigued (low) to elated (high), and negative emotions range from sadness (low) to violent rage (high) (high).

1. Shoulder and Torso: hunching the houlder and leaning forward is associated with intense anger. In conclusion, leaning backward can be a sign of panic or fear. If they stand up traight with their houlder back and head held high, they feel confident. However, if they hunch their shoulders or lump forward, they are looking for ympathy, bored, or feel nervous.

2. Arm and Hand: If they are sad, they will likely place their arm next to their side and put their hand in their pocket. If they are annoyed or irritated, they may place one arm on their side or hips and gesticulate with their opposing hand (pointing or flat palm). If they are indifferent or do not care, they will place their hands behIND their back.

3. Leg and Feet: If they hake their leg or tap their toes, they may be anxiou, annoyed, or hurry. However, some people naturally hake their leg while sitting without it meaning anything.

3. Look for "Fight Or Flight" Signs: When something unexpected occurs, whether good or bad, it stimulates a part of the brain that is outside of our direct control. This results in physiological responses such as dilated pupils, rapid breathing, increased weating, and increased heart rate. [42] You can tell if someone is nervous, treed, or anxious by looking for signs such as weaty palms or armpits, red or flushed face, or haking hand.

1. When men are upset or treed, they tend to how ign of aggreion, frustration, and anger. Women, on the other hand, may become more talkative or seek social support. Some men and women become more withdrawn and q uiet when experiencing negative emotion depending on their peronality.

4. know how they are feeling: Sometimes being direct is the best way to read emotion. While other people may lie and say they're fine when they aren't, it never hurts to ask. You can also use their response to read between the lines by noting the tone of voice combined with facial expression and body language. You can also look for specific verbal cues that indicate how they feel inide. For example, if they are bored or ad, they would speak lower and at a lower fre q uency. If they are excited or upset, the peed and fre q uency of their voice will increase.

1. Try speaking to them individually rather than in a group. They may be more open and truthful about their emotions if they are with a trusted friend or family member.

CHAPTER 7:

ELEMENTS OF COMMUNICATION

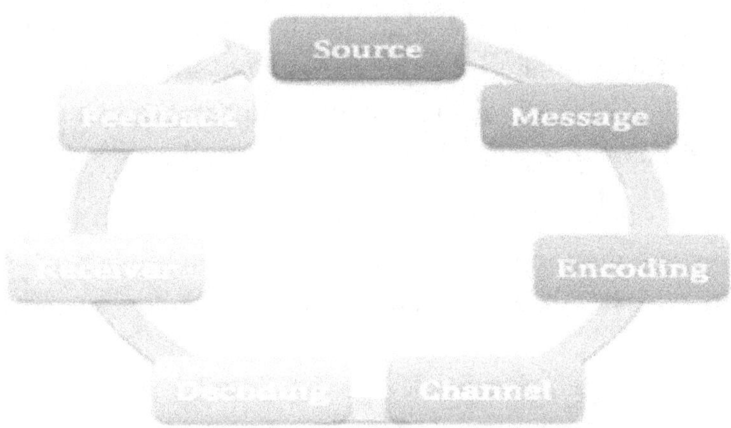

Effective communication entails much more than just the exchange of information; it entails comprehending the intent and emotion underlying a discussion, which necessitates active participation from everyone involved. Both individuals must pay attention to ensure that the message is being conveyed in an intended manner. Active listening is required to help an individual feel understood and heard. When it comes to your practice or buiness, a team with topnotch communication knowledge will prove valuable in more than a few aspects. Communication is the conveying of meage by exchanging thoughts or information via speech, visuals, signals, writing, or behaviour. Communication necessitates a sender, a message, and a recipient, though the receiver may not be present or aware of the sender's intent to communicate Effective communication necessitates a combination of abilities, including:

- Stress management (at the time)
- Appropriate nonverbal communication/Body language
- Engaged litening
- The ability to effectively communicate with self-confidence
- The ability to identify and comprehend the emotions of all individuals involved in the communication (including your own)

Tip for Improved Communication

1.Manage Stress In The Moment To Improve Communication

Individuals who feel emotionally overwhelmed or treed are more likely to miinterpret conversations, end confusing nonverbal ignal, and lape into unhealthy, mind

Learn How To Recognize Stress Symptoms:

- tense mucle
- handclent handclent handclent
- Slow breathing or forgetting to breathe

Solutions:

- Take time after the conversation to calm down and re-examine the conversation.
- Pause to try and de-tre: Cloe your eye, take few deep, cleaning breathers, and relax your mucle.
- Find a quiet place to meditate.

2.Appropriate Nonverbal Communication / Body Language

Nonverbal communication must reinforce—rather than contradict—what is being discussed. When you say one thing and your body shows another, liteners may wonder if you're telling the

103

truth. For example, if you begin discussing how happy you are with a taff member's ability to take a month off and travel the world, but your hand are folded in front of you and you avoid making eye contact, you are

Solutions:

- Avoid sending negative nonverbal communications (tapping your foot, crossing your arm, and looking away) because doing so may cause the other person to become defensive.
- Concentrate on using open body language, such as uncrossing your arms, sitting on the edge of your chair, and maintaining good eye contact.
- Use your body language to emphaize and enhance your conversation. smiling while patting a taff member on the houlder to congratulate him or her on a promotion I a great way to ue your body language to accentuate

3.Listening Engaged

Communication necessitates engaged listening; thus, planning your next entence, checking email and text messages, or simply thinking

What you want for lunch interferes with your ability to focus. Staying focused from one moment to the next ensures that you do not miss any of the nonverbal cues used during the conversation.

Solutions:

- Concentrate on the here and now during discussions.
- Allow the speaker to know you're listening by using small gestures such as nodding your head or short verbal responses.

104

- Pay attention to the ubtle change in the speaker's voice, as well as his or her body language and other nonverbal cues. These actions reveal how the person feels and what they are attempting to communicate with you.
- When you find it difficult to concentrate on a conversation, repeat the words in your head. This will reinforce their message and make it easier for you to stay focused.
- Do not interrupt or attempt to reroute the conversation to address your concerns.
- Favouring your right ear can help you pick up on the ubtle emotional nuance an individual I portraying. This tip works because the right ear is connected to the left side of the brain, which contains the main processing centres for emotion and comprehension. Try standing (or sitting) straight with your chin down and tilting your right ear toward the person speaking.

4.Self-Confidence Display

Playing elf-confidence with assertive expreion clarifies communication. xpre ideas in an open and honest format. The goal of effective communication is not to impose your opinions on others or to win an argument; rather, it is to understand others.

Solutions:

- Experiencing ager is fine; just respect others and try to find a positive way to communicate how you feel.
- Realize that your thoughts are just as important as everyone else's.
- The ability to identify and comprehend all of the emotions associated with a given situation.

While communication skills are a major factor of good communication throughout a business, communication avenues are econd only to the ability to communicate. Our team chat feature make interoffice communication eamle. You can learn more about it here. Use your communication skills to build trust with taff members, clients, and colleagues. Strong communication increases positive outcomes, helps to boost morale, and eases tension in the workplace.

Effective Communication Requires 10 esential Skills

Being able to communicate effectively is an essential skill. Whether it's in our business or our relationships, effective communication is the key to our success. Life coaching for effective communication I a fantastic way to learn and attain the kil. I'll show you how to get ahead and keep ahead ahead ahead ahead ahead ahead ahead ahead ahead ahead ahead ahead ahead ahead ahea Here are my ten eential knowledge Make these kills now, and they'll serve you well for a long time to come!

1.Listening

Being a good litener is one of the most important aspects of effective communication. People dislike communicating with others who are only interested in telling them what they want to tell them and are not interested in what you have to say. Effective communication necessitates active listening, so practice active listening until it becomes second nature to you.

So, what exactly is ctive listening? ACTIVE litening entails hearing and comprehending what a person is saying to you. You cannot respond appropriately unless you clearly understand what a person is saying to you. Gain clarification by aking q uetion or rephrase.

What you're being told, so you're sure you fully understand the message that's being conveyed to you.

For example, you could say, "So, what you're saying is..."

2.Communication Non-Verbal

The words we choose the account for only 7% of the messages being conveyed, making nonverbal communication all the more important. Body language is a vital communication tool. Your body language should assist you in conveying your words. Another factor to consider is the tone of your voice, your hand gestures, and maintaining eye contact. If you are relaxed and have a friendly tone, peron will be encouraged to peak openly with you. Adopt an open tance position, with relaxed leg and open arm. You must maintain eye contact with the person with whom you are communicating, but be careful not to stare at them, as this is simply inconvenient. It is simply critical that you recognize the non-verbal signal being displayed by the other person. These signs will give you an idea of how that person is feeling.

3.Be CLear and Concise

Convey your message in as few words as possible. Convey your message, concisely, and directly, whether in person, over the phone, or via email. If you are exceptional with your words, the listener will either lose focus or simply be unconcerned about what you want. Before speaking, give some thought to the message you want to convey. This will keep you from rambling and confusing.

4,Be Prononable

When communicating face to face with someone, use a friendly tone with a simple mile and ask a personal q uetion. These things encourage the other person to engage in honest, open communication. When using written communication (e.g., email), you can achieve thiever by adding a smile personal message, for example, "How was your weekend?"

5.Be Confident

Confidence underpins all effective communication. Other people will believe you will do what you say if you appear confident. Making eye contact, using a firm but the friendly tone (never aggressive), are all ways to exude confidence. Remember to always pay attention to the other person and look for nonverbal cues.

6.Empathy

mpathy is the deal of being able to undertand and hare the feeling of another peron. Even if you disagree with the person with whom you are communicating, you must understand and respect their point of view. Simply saying to that person, "I understand what you're saying," will let them know that you've been listening to them and respect their point of view.

Always have an Open Mind

Being an effective communicator necessitates that every converation I approached with a flexible, open mind. This isn't always easy to achieve, but it's critical for effective communication.

108

Always engage in active listening, and be sure to demonstrate empathy by acknowledging that you understand the other person's point of view. Adopting this approach will always ensure honest, productive communication.

8.Convey Repect

Other people will be more likely to communicate with you if you respect them and their ideas. Simply addressing another person by name will make them feel appreciated. When communicating via telephone, keep focued on the converation and avoid being distracted in any way. When communicating via email, take the time to complete and edit your meage, taking care to addre the recipient by name.

9.Feedback give and receive

Giving and receiving appropriate feedback is an essential communication skill, especially for those of us whose roles include managing others. Providing constructive feedback as well as a Giving someone praise can greatly increase motivation and build morale. It's just as important that you accept and encourage feedback from others. liten to feedback and act poitively on it always. If you are unsure about any aspect of the feedback, simply ask a question to obtain clarification from the other person.

10.Consider the best medium for the job!

The final item on my list is determining the best mode of communication to use. Being mindful of using the best form of communication will result in a positive response. Consider who you're trying to communicate with, how important the topic is, and how valuable that person is. For example, asking your bo for a raie I never going to be taken eriouly if you do it by text — so consider what's appropriate!

CHAPTER 8:

EMOTIONAL INTELLIGENCE